DYSFUNCTIONAL INSPIRATION

ARTHUR GREENO

Published by Expert Message Group, LLC

Expert Message Group, LLC
P.O. Box 949
Tulsa, OK 74101

415.523.0404

www.expertmessagegroup.com

First Printing, May 2012

ISBN 9781936875047

Printed in Canada
Set in Book Antiqua 11.5/16

For permissions, please contact:

Expert Message Group, LLC
P.O. Box 949
Tulsa, OK 74101

This book is dedicated to my wife Noell, who has told me from our first date I had a story to tell. You were right, and I was wrong.

To my kids - Connor, Casey, Chase, Cameron, Savannah, and Sydney - incredible things are at your fingertips, you are the only one who can decide if they're yours for the taking.

To my friends: if you make fun of anything in this book, next time I will write one and make fun of you (you know I will).

Sometimes it's not
always about winning-

It's about
having FUN,
and making memories

CHAPTER 1
THE MAN BEHIND THE WORLD'S (ALMOST) LARGEST SNO-CONE

Big Dreams instill passion in others, while nay-sayers still sit alone and complain.

-Arthur Greeno

I t was anything but an ordinary February day in Tulsa.

For one thing, it was five degrees outside. Now if you live in Minnesota or North Dakota or Alaska that might sound downright balmy for a day in February. But in Tulsa, where the average February temperature is nicely-above freezing, weather that cold qualifies as a pretty major event.

And it wasn't just cold, it was snowy. We'd had 24 inches the week before, and then another 12 the previous day. There was snow everywhere — on my lawn, on the sidewalks, and piled up in giant drifts averaging 3-4 feet tall all over the parking lot of the stand-alone Chick-fil-A business I own and operate.

It looked kind of like the North Pole — that is, if the North Pole was located in the middle of the plains of Oklahoma, with Santa perched behind the wheel of a John Deere tractor…

Anyway, most people, if they know what's good for them, would opt to spend a five-degree day inside, curled up under a blanket, sipping a hot chocolate in front of a roaring fire — or at least a decent space heater.

But I'm not "most people." My name is Arthur Greeno, and as you'll learn over the course of the next hundred or so pages, I'm what some people might refer to as a "goofball." Or "a little bit wacky."

You know… nuts. There's one of me in pretty much every group of guys. That one guy who makes you think, "Arthur would definitely do this," or "My buddy Arthur has a 5-foot fiberglass replica of SpongeBob Squarepants." You know… *that* guy.

And on this particular five-degree Oklahoma Thursday, being the "out there" kinda guy that I am, I had some pretty big plans. My parking lot was full of snow! To me, that only meant one thing…

Sno-cones.

In my town and in the world of Chick-fil-A, I'm known as the "Big Event Guy." Whenever there's an excuse for a no-holds-barred spectacle, anything from an unseasonably cold winter day to the Fourth of July, you can pretty much count on me to make something crazy happen.

I've brought a herd of live cows to my Chick-fil-A parking lot to greet guests as they walk in. I celebrated the launch of The Chick-fil-A Spicy Chicken Biscuit by buying my own, personal fire truck and driving it around town complete with a fiberglass cow in a fireman suit. And when there's no real event to celebrate… well, no problem. I make up my own special occasions by putting on a different theme night at my restaurants, where we decorate every inch of the store with a theme — Bugs Night, Under the Sea Night, Space Night, and our most popular one, Superhero Night- a new one every month.

Over-the-top, crazy events are pretty much what I'm all about — so, of course, there have been *many*. In fact, some of these events have been so big, they've even resulted in world records being set!

Google my name and you'll see what I mean. *The World's Largest Sweet Tea* was created by me. *The World's Largest Lemonade?* Me again. You'll also find my name if you look up *World's Largest Hand-Spun Milkshake*, although, that one wasn't an official Guinness World

Record. However, it did make it into one of the *Ripley's Believe it or Not* books. And it was definitely the biggest shake Tulsa had ever seen...

So with all that snow just sitting there in my Chick-fil-A parking lot, it shouldn't come as a surprise that my thoughts automatically turned to sno-cones. Specifically, this: was there enough snow right there in the lot to break yet another world record?

I was about to find out.

We decided Thursday, February 10 would be the big day — the date itself was not special, but we knew we had another big snowfall on its way. However, since I was not (yet!) an expert in sno-cone construction, I brought in someone who was — Josh Juarez from Josh's Sno Shack, a guy who had worked for me for a time while he was in high school. I joined with Josh and his crack team of sno-cone builders, and together, after some prep work (getting the giant cup, massive amounts of syrup and giant sprayers to shoot it), we spent that day packing the frosty stuff into an enormous cup and covering it with colorful, yummy syrup sweet enough to make Scrooge himself smile. We also used similar sprayers filled with dye to paint the snow mounds, transforming the parking lot of my quick service restaurant into a rainbow wonderland.

We had plenty of company on hand to watch the spectacle. The local media, having been alerted in advance that the crazy Chick-fil-A guy was at it again, showed up in force. So did about 500 other people who crowded my chilly parking lot to witness the event and warmed up inside with free hot chocolate and hot Spicy Chicken Biscuits.

When we were finished, we didn't break the record — we were about 3-feet short — but we definitely had a blast trying. Not only that, but we did some amazing business. 500 guests is not a bad turnout for a below-freezing February Thursday at a Tulsa quick service restaurant. Making the whole event, by every standard *except* the one set by the fine folks at Guinness, a resounding success.

It also, in a roundabout way, brings me to why I wrote this book. In Tulsa, and especially in the world of Chick-fil-A, I'm known for crazy stunts, but also for having a pretty successful business operation. I'll admit right now, I've been incredibly lucky along my path. I'm one of the few franchisees to whom Chick-fil-A has granted a license to own and operate two restaurant businesses (more on that later). Of course, I'll be the first to say that it's not all me—I owe a lot of that privilege to my amazing team that allows me to be in two places at once… *almost!*

On the personal front, I've also been lucky. I've been married for 18 years to Noell, a woman who is not only absolutely smokin' hot, but also loves me anyway! We've got six great kids, which, okay, some people might not regard as a good thing, but we kinda like the chaos. We've got a nice, comfortable home, great friends, and a lifestyle I imagine some might describe as "enviable."

I will be the first to admit it. I am very, very blessed.

But there's one very small problem with being so blessed. It can sometimes give people the wrong impression, or the wrong idea about me.

The fact that I'm successful in business and also kind of a wacky, fun-loving guy without a lot of obvious stresses or problems presents a certain image.

Some people who don't know me automatically assume that I've had it easy, both in business and in life. They assume that I'm one of those people who was born into the "right" family, went to the "right" schools and had a good, easy path basically laid out in front of me.

I want to make this clear: it's not that I care if people think I'm lucky—I am! (In fact, I feel the harder I've worked, the luckier I've gotten). What worries me is that when people see me, they think that what I have is unattainable to "regular people" like them.

And *that* is why I'm sitting here writing this right now… instead of making plans to build the World's Largest Chicken Biscuit (and my team thanks me for this).

I want you—and everyone—to know that if I could make it, anyone can.

You can.

The fact is, while the life I live right now is definitely wonderful, things have not always been easy for me. If you had asked my parents, grandparents or anyone who knew me growing up—heck, if you asked *me*—where I would end up in life, this is definitely not the future they would have had in mind, not even close.

Because, like a lot of people today, maybe even like you, I didn't grow up with much. A lot of the time, I was lucky to have a roof over my head or food on my table. It wouldn't be a stretch to describe my childhood as difficult.

And the term "awful" wouldn't be too far off at times.

But the thing is, even back then, I was *still* blessed.

I just didn't know it.

Because all that time I was struggling, all that time that I spent feeling like I was on the outside looking in, *inside* me was everything I needed to build a different kind of life—both for myself and for my children. *Inside* of me was the ability to succeed, to achieve happiness, to have peace.

And the really, really good news is, wherever you are in life right now, those very same keys are inside you. All you need to do is find them—and like any good athlete knows, the more you use them, the stronger they become.

So that, in a nutshell, is why I'm writing this book. Maybe, by sharing my story with you, I can give you a perspective that if you try hard enough, if you help enough people, if you never, ever give up, hitting that goal, no matter how large or small, really is possible.

Maybe, as you read through these pages, you'll find the inspiration to look at your own challenges in a different way. Maybe you'll realize that, whatever has happened in your past, your future is still right up ahead of you. It's beautiful and exciting—and worth fighting for.

Or maybe you'll just be inspired to build a really big sno-cone.

Either way, I've got some stories to tell you. So let's get started.

You have the ability to inspire
others just by being you, I do.
I remember watching
someone in school and I
loved their handwriting.
In fact, I copied the way
they did their A's and it
is part of my signature to
this day.

We influence people daily
whether it's in person, on
the phone or social media,
be yourself.

CHAPTER 2
STRANGER IN PARADISE

I was born in Chicago, Illinois on June 20, 1969 (feel free to send me a birthday card if you want). My dad was a math professor and a pretty imposing guy—6 foot 3 and about 225 lbs. The old pictures show him with black, short hair, but I remember him as balding in the middle.

Dad was a strong, outdoorsy person who loved to camp, canoe, and fish. But at home, he was just like one of those professors in the movies—he always had dry erase boards around his home office with equations scrawled all over them, as well as dice, flash cards, overhead projectors, piles of books, papers, all kinds of professor paraphernalia.

Mom was about 5 foot 5, skinny, with long black hair. She was very beautiful when she was younger…although as she got older, her lifestyle would take its toll.

Me, I was very much the middle child—I had a sister named Lorine, who was two years older than me, and a sister named Kathleen, who was two years younger. So I was kind of the odd man out.

Religion was not a big deal in my family. We said we were Catholic, but we only went to church twice a year—for the big events—Christmas and Easter. Beyond that, God wasn't much of a presence in our lives. And, being only six, this didn't seem particularly strange to me.

Honestly, I don't really remember a lot from those first six years of my life. My dad tells one story that sticks with me. I had gone to a preschool that was down the street from my house, close enough to walk to. When I got old enough for kindergarten, it was at a different school that was also close enough to walk to, but in a different direction. Well, apparently I liked the preschool better, because one day I walked there instead of walking to kindergarten, like I was supposed to.

As you might imagine, the kindergarten freaked, the preschool freaked, my mom freaked…but hey! I guess, even at that very young age, I was already developing the ability to go after what I wanted in life—even if it wasn't the "normal" thing to do…

Life went on like that for a while, just normal kid stuff, until I was 7 or 8 years old. Then, everything changed. Because that's the year we moved to Hawaii.

The State of Hawaii offered my dad what seemed like an incredible opportunity—to revolutionize the way they taught math in our almost-brand-new 50th state.

News that we were moving to Paradise didn't blow me away. I didn't really understand the difference between Hawaii and Chicago—I had no concept of "Paradise"—so I wasn't especially excited. In fact, I was a little teed off that I was being forced to leave my best friend Stanley behind and cross most of a continent and an ocean to live in an entirely new place where I'd never, ever been.

The rest of my family, on the other hand, was over the moon.

We were leaving the Windy City and moving to Paradise! Trading below-zero temperatures and snowdrifts for palm trees and ocean breezes! What could possibly be bad about that?

We would find out soon enough.

(This would be a good time to start playing the theme from *Jaws*.)

(And speaking of that, try living in Hawaii in 1975—the year *Jaws* was released. I saw it when I was about 8. And still managed to go in the ocean anyway, but every time a fish bumped me, I would scream like an 5-year-old little girl.)

But getting back to the move…I don't know if it happened while we were suspended in mid-air somewhere over the Pacific Ocean or sometime later (I'm guessing probably later, but the idea of it happening in mid-air feels so much more dramatic). Anyway, in an almost staggering example of bad timing — after we had left our home in Chicago and packed all our stuff and left jobs and spent thousands of dollars to get us and our possessions across America and the Pacific, and left the mainland behind — my dad's job was eliminated.

I don't really know the details, but to my understanding — Poof! Just like that, it was gone — before his chair had a chance to get warm.

The five of us were basically stranded in Paradise.

Actually, "stranded" was the operative word. We couldn't afford to pack everything up again and go back to Chicago.

My dad started a math tutoring agency — which was pretty much all a displaced math professor could do on the island of Oahu — all while searching for the "real job" in his field of expertise that would make everything okay again. Except there wasn't much of a demand for math tutoring in Hawaii back in the '70s. (Maybe it should have been a sign that the job that brought us there in the first place didn't even exist anymore?)

So it was left to my mom, who was both a registered nurse and a medical transcriptionist, to take over the role as the family breadwinner. And unfortunately, this was not a role she appeared to enjoy.

Maybe it was the stress of suddenly having to be responsible for paying the bills, or anger at my dad for losing his job, or loneliness at being so far away from home. I really don't know, I was six years old — basically all I knew was that things were messed up! But my mom started drinking. Actually, I later found out she had always been a drinker, but her consumption definitely increased. And her behavior definitely changed. Maybe it was the drinking, or maybe it changed because she was working, or tired from working. All I knew is that suddenly, my mom seemed a lot less interested in my sisters and me. She would come home from work with a new case of beer, sit down in the kitchen alone and drink or smoke for the rest of the night.

It's probably not surprising that, with all those changes, she and my dad started fighting. All the fun and happiness was gone, like somebody popped our happiness balloon.

We became a different kind of family. For example—you know those family dinners where everyone sits around the table and talks about their day, and laughs and tells inside jokes in between passing the green beans and the chicken? We used to have those when I was younger. In the '70s, we lived in a house with a wall of mirrors, and I would get in so much trouble at dinner making faces at myself (in fact, people still tease me because of the faces I make!). But as time went on, there was less face-making, less laughing, until the only sound left was the sound of chewing. Eventually, the whole idea of the "family dinner" pretty much disappeared.

I also had a strangely nervous stomach. Of course, that gave me the enviable (for a school-age boy) skill of being able to pass gas almost on demand—but we'll get to my gastrointestinal issues later...

The real problems at my house didn't start until after my sisters and I went to bed. Thinking we were asleep and therefore unaware (I wish!), that's when my parents would finally let out all their frustrations with each other and our situation and fight.

Now, almost all parents fight, I realize that. Couples are going to disagree, problems are going to happen. What was different in my house was the *way* my parents fought—like they were in some sort of contest where the object was to make the most noise possible.

Sometimes it came in the form of yelling a lot of angry words—many that my children have never, ever heard. Other times, there would be slamming doors and smashing dishes. And sometimes—way, way more often than I'd like to remember—the fights would end with sirens and flashing lights...when the police would come.

Six-year-old boys love policemen—but not when they show up at their house in the middle of the night! It was pretty scary stuff.. Although, I think what's scarier is that, after awhile, my sisters and I got used to it. We didn't talk about it. But we got used to it. It became our "normal."

I really had no one to turn to to talk about the situation. Besides, even if I did have someone to talk to, I had no idea how to approach the subject. I was a six-year-old kid who was new in town—not to mention in that part of the world. I had no friends, no extended family, no church and basically nowhere to turn for support.

If I knew then what I know now, I would have asked God to help me. Actually, I did—many times—but it was more along the lines of, "Please God, make it go away." I tried to bargain with Him, offering to give up things like comic books, or lying, or TV…anything to make things better.

But I didn't need to bargain. He was with me every step of the way. I just didn't know it.

That fall, I finally got out of the house when I started school with my sisters. Which ushered in a new era—life as The New Kid. In Hawaii, they called me the "main-lander," because I came from the mainland (duh!) and also a "Haole," which basically meant "white man" or foreigner. Neither was really that bad when it comes to kid insults. Except that they always had rumors of a "Kill Haole Day" on the last day of school, and those were scary enough that my mom would actually keep us home. There were always stories of how some Haole kid got beat up, or disappeared.

However, being new in town, and from the fabled Mainland, wasn't all that set me apart from the crowd. Since my dad still hadn't found a "real job" in the math field and my mom didn't make much money, we were what you might call a "lower income family." That meant that at school, I got these shiny tokens, which I traded in for lunch. I thought being able to buy my lunch with these cool, shiny pieces of metal meant I was special.

But the other kids knew what those tokens meant.

And even worse, they knew that I was *that* kid from *that* house— the one with the yelling parents and the loud noises and the police cars that kept showing up late at night.

So I made very few friends at school—and felt lonely and awkward. Not really surprising.

What was surprising is what I did *after* school. I don't know what possessed me to do it, but in the afternoons, when other kids were on play dates or home doing their homework, I became a door-to-door salesman. And the product I was selling was *me!*

I would actually march up to strangers' doors, ring the bell and ask the mom or whoever else opened the door if they had any boys my age I could play with. And, as I remember it, I had very little fear. Outside school walls, I had developed quite an outgoing personality when I needed it.

I don't remember making any big "sales" on my rounds. I imagine most of the grown-ups were not impressed by my underage moxie — what kind of child goes door-to-door looking for friends? Where was his mother? But I do think it shows something unique about me. I was learning to take care of myself — to identify what I wanted and go after it.

Eventually, the kids at school started getting bolder about what was happening at my house. This meant that instead of staring and pointing, kids — especially our friends — started asking questions. "Why were the police at your house?" "Did they take anyone to jail?" We were famous…but for all the wrong reasons. I even got into a few fights over my family's notoriety.

It's not like I was living under a rock (even if I was on an island in the middle of the ocean). This was the '70s! Although our tiny TV eventually got stolen, I did know about *The Brady Bunch* and *Happy Days* — and they reminded me that my family was, very clearly, not normal. The cops didn't show up at the Brady's house in the middle of the night!

But when you're a little kid, what you experience every day tends to become normal for you. I didn't really understand what it would be like to live any other way. So I managed to live *my* life in a way that felt normal to me. I did things that other kids did — I got involved in sports, joined Cub Scouts and did my best to fit in.

And just when it seemed like I was getting settled and developing a routine, it would all fall apart.

Because we'd have to move.

Moving was the one of the defining experiences of my childhood. Before fifth grade, I went to four different elementary schools just in Hawaii. The problem was my mom and her jobs—she kept getting fired. I guess that's what happens when you don't show up for work all the time, your boss eventually catches on and replaces you with someone who will!

This was a bigger problem for me and my little world of "normal" because my mom usually worked at hospitals. Now, in Hawaii, at least at that time, there was usually only one hospital in an area. So every time my mom got a new job, we'd have to move to a new place. My dad still hadn't found any work that could support the family, so we basically had no choice. If we wanted to eat, we had to move.

This could be why I didn't really learn very much in school— although there's also the possibility that I was a little bit lazy. One good thing about having parents who don't nag you about your homework, at least from a kid's point of view…is that *you don't have to do your homework!* When your parents don't care about school, they don't punish you for doing badly in school. So while my teachers yelled and complained about my failure to do what I was supposed to, my parents were too busy with their own problems to worry about it.

However, I did have some problems that even my overtaxed parents couldn't overlook. By the time I was 10, I was getting really bad, serious stomachaches on a regular basis. At first, my parents shrugged it off as normal "kid griping"—they probably thought I was eating too much candy or didn't want dinner or something like that.

But it just kept going. So eventually, since my mother was a nurse, she realized that there might be something more going on than too many junk food binges and took me to a doctor.

What happened next was one of the scariest experiences of my life. This doctor literally strapped me down to a table to examine me. Imagine how scary that was—I was 10 years old, strapped to a table in a doctor's office and had no idea what was coming next! The doctor did the usual doctor thing, "relax, this won't hurt a bit…" and promised it was only going to be "uncomfortable."

If, by uncomfortable, you mean *excruciating*! Now I know why they strapped me down. First, the doctor stuck a tube down my throat that had a little camera on it—which, had the camera-tube not been *shoved down my throat,* would have been kinda cool. But then the doctor pumped air down my throat into my stomach so the camera could see. My stomach didn't like that, so I kept letting out these tremendous belches!

Anyway, had I not been strapped down, I would have hit the ceiling! (By the way, you know on cartoons when people get filled up with air, and then when they stop filling them with air they fly around the room? It does not happen. Just so you know.)

The good news was, my torture session was enough to establish that there was, in fact, something real wrong with me.

I had stomach ulcers.

Yes, at the age of 10, *I had ulcers!* Like a 45-year-old, Type-A businessman going through his second divorce. That just doesn't happen…

The doctor felt that way too, so he asked my parents if I'd been under any "unusual stress…"

"Unusual" being the operative word—this was pretty much the same stress I'd been through all the time!

Anyway, to my parents' credit, they tried. They changed my diet, I guess hoping some really bland food might counteract all the moving and other drama I'd been going through.

If you haven't by now, at some point, you're probably going to think, "That poor kid! Didn't he have *any* fun in Hawaii?" I promise, I'm not telling you all this stuff so you'll feel sorry for me. Remember the sno-cone! It gets better, I promise!

Besides, kids being kids, there was always time for some sort of fun. Kathleen and I would spend a lot of time doing stuff together— Lorine was getting older and had older friends, so she would spend her time with them. So Kathleen and I would make up games and hang out together. One summer we were playing in her room—I think because it was on the other side of the house from where my dad would tutor people. Well, every day, we noticed her room would stink more and more, a horrible rotten smell. It got so bad that at one point our eyes were watering. So we decided whatever was behind the stench, we were going to find it. We tore through her room—I think we spent hours going through every inch of space. And after a few hours... we found it.

It was an Easter egg, leftover from April.

It was black, stinky, rotten and absolutely disgusting! When Kathleen found it I got real close and took a big, deep whiff—and almost barfed! Of course we threw it out, laughing so hard we cried—but I can't remember if we were crying because it smelled so bad, or if it was because of how funny it was.

After smelling an egg like that you would think I would have learned, however I guess it takes a couple times for me to learn. Later, in high school, I was picking out some shampoo. I was wondering what it smelled like. So I opened it up, put my nose right up to it and took a whiff. Nothing. I gently took a whiff while squeezing it. It shot straight up my nose, so far up, I could taste it in my mouth. It also burned, and I had to find a bathroom and flush my nasal canal out. At the same time I wanted to scratch my face off due to the pain and itching in my head. That's when I learned to take whiffs a little more cautiously.

Being in Hawaii, I also had some incredible adventures. Especially when we were living in this one apartment complex where the groundskeeper liked to hang out with all of the kids in the community.

I know that wouldn't go over too well these days—but this was the '70s (or maybe the very early '80s by this point) and nobody worried about stuff like that. And, more importantly, it was fine. *He* was fine. And he gave me my best memory of all my years in Hawaii.

It happened one day when he invited a bunch of us to hike up to a waterfall. I think five or six boys went, it was a pretty major hike, but when you're that age, you don't think twice about an adventure!

So we came out of the foresty part and in this clearing before the top, and we could see these older kids jumping from the top of waterfall, screaming and laughing all the way down until they hit the *very* narrow pool of water that was at the bottom.

To my twelve-year-old self, it looked awesome. Terrifying, but awesome.

Well, at that point, the groundskeeper made us all a little bet. Whoever followed those big kids and jumped off the top of the waterfall would get a Big Mac at McDonald's.

A Big Mac? I was in.

(And if I was willing to risk my life for a Big Mac, imagine how far I would have gone for a Chick-fil-A Sandwich???)

How often did I get to eat a real, genuine Big Mac? My parents didn't have money for stuff like that.

I made my way to the top of the falls. The older kids parted like the Red Sea, letting the little guy make his way through. Looking back, I don't know if they were laughing at me or encouraging me to go for it. But I didn't care. I had my eyes on the prize.

Then I got to the edge and looked down. Yikes! That pool was TINY. There were jagged rocks at the bottom. I could die!

Yeah…but if I made it…I would be biting into a Big Mac.

I jumped.

For what seemed like a minute or more, I was in a state of suspended animation. I looked at the rocks. I looked at the tiny pool.

I was seized with complete and utter panic.

Frantic, I started waving my arms to beat back against the air. My hands flailed around looking for something, anything to grab on to (I think that was the day I mastered how to scream like a high-pitched little girl). And almost as soon as it began, I hit the water, hard. My entire body stung as I made for the surface, popped my head up for air and thought…

Big Mac!

It was the best burger I ever tasted.

Actually, everyone in our group scored a Big Mac, whether they jumped or not. I think the groundskeeper felt just a *little* guilty from the red marks I had all over my body…

But red marks and pain or no, that day, I learned something very important. There's nothing as empowering as taking a giant risk and succeeding. Suddenly, you feel like, if you want something badly enough, you can do anything.

Unfortunately, I didn't add the word "legal" to the end of that thought…

Please note: at one point, years later, my wife Noell and I were in Hawaii on a vacation. We decided to go to that waterfall. When she saw how high it was, and how small the pool was that I had I jumped into, she slapped me right in the middle of the chest. Not knowing exactly what I had done this time, I asked her "What was that for?" She replied "You could have killed yourself!" The red handprint is still smack in the middle of my chest to this day.

Around that time, when I was 12 or so, there was nothing bigger in the kid world than *Star Wars*. Just about every kid I knew had a collection of *Star Wars* figurines, or at least I felt like they did. I wanted one so badly I could taste it — kind of like that Big Mac — but there was no waterfall I could jump off, no dare I could meet that would put one in my hand.

My parents weren't going to buy me one — at least not until Christmas or my birthday, which I assume, based on what I did next, had to be very far off.

Yes, once again, I took matters into my own hands. I stole a Luke Skywalker figurine.

It wasn't exactly premeditated or anything. If it had been, maybe I would have thought about who might be watching me in that comic book store, or what might happen next.

And it's not like I didn't know that what I was doing was against the law, and at least technically, *wrong*. I just didn't care. I took Luke Skywalker, stuffed him in my pocket and headed for the door.

Which is when the fun began…

I felt a strong, male hand grab me — it dragged me through the store, back to the office and threw me against a desk. It was the owner. And he was *very angry.*

He smelled like beer and cigarettes (at least that's how I remember him) and his face was so red and his neck veins so bulgy he looked to me like he might explode. He was also Chinese, and when he yelled at me, some of the words were in Chinese! Which, in retrospect, was probably a good thing...

Somehow, I think it was reflex, I was still clutching Luke. But the owner obviously knew it was there and demanded I hand it over — which I was more than happy to do. I just wanted to get out of there.

But he wasn't done with me.

Today, I don't know of a storeowner who could get away with this. But this particular storeowner had no fear of "the authorities" or parents calling in a lawyer. As I headed for the door, he yanked me back into the office and doled out what he felt was appropriate punishment, slapping me, kicking me, screaming at me and swearing at me like he was a complete, raging lunatic.

I've never been so scared in my life. In fact, have you ever heard the term, "scared the crap out of me?" I am living proof that this phenomenon is actually possible. Because, there, in the back of the store with the crazed store owner possibly preparing to kill me, I pooped my pants. I walked home after that remembering what it was like when I was four years old — the last time I had pooped my pants. I remembered that it was not comfortable.

I was lucky to escape with my life — dirty pants or not. But it still didn't scare me straight.

After a few days, I looked back on the incident and played it over and over in my mind. I decided that my big mistake was not "Breaking the Law," but "Poor Planning." How could I have failed to look around and see if anyone was watching me? Of course I got caught!

With my *next* target, I reasoned, I'd do things right.

When that time came, I set my sights on something simpler — a candy bar at a convenience store. I played it cool, walking in with my head down, hands in my pockets. I eyed the storeowner warily.

Then, when he looked away, I snatched the candy bar.

Nothing happened. I was home free. I sauntered, as nonchalantly as I could, toward the door. I was just about to taste sweet freedom — to tear open that wrapper and bite down on the spoils of my victory — when I felt a hand firmly grab my arm.

It wasn't the owner. It was a cop!

He actually handcuffed me and sat me in the back of the squad car for the long ride to the station, where he called my parents. As expected, they didn't make an enormous stink about what had happened; they were too busy with their own problems to worry about their son stealing a candy bar (and, since the comic book store owner preferred beating me up to turning me in, they didn't know about the infamous Luke Skywalker event). So basically, I was free to steal again.

But for some reason, I didn't. Something inside me changed that day. I don't know why or where it came from, but I lost the urge to steal. Maybe it was the look of disappointment on my mom's face. Or maybe, I decided it just wasn't worth it.

So I went straight.

Once you finally have
a resolute decision to
make a change in your
life, the universe will
unleash powers that will
come against you!
Stay strong...
Make it happen!

I know we feel like we
are alone, but no man is an
island to himself.

CHAPTER 3
THE DAY MY HAIR FROZE– AND OTHER STORIES OF A YEAR IN CHICAGO

Don't cry because it's over. Smile because it happened.
— Unknown proverb

My criminal career now behind me, life in Hawaii continued as normal—or, more like normal for my family.

At this point, things started to change.

My mom lost another job.

I realize that on the surface, that might not sound like anything special as far as Greeno Family Problems are concerned. My mom had lost jobs before. And every time she lost a job, she would eventually find another one.

Except, this last job that she lost also happened to be The Very Last Available Hospital Job on Oahu—at least for my mom.

Remember in the last chapter, when I told you that there were only so many hospitals on Oahu?

Well, at this point, my mom had already worked for just about all of those hospitals. Which meant there was no one left who would hire her. And since my dad's situation hadn't changed and that math professor's dream job had never materialized, we were left with only one option.

My mom had to call *her parents*.

Imagine what it would feel like, as an adult, to crawl back to Mom and Dad for help? Actually, in my mom's case, it was Mom and Stepdad. The good news was, they stepped up and offered to let us live with them back in Chicago. They even bought our tickets back to the mainland.

The bad news was, my grandparents were not big fans of my father. They blamed him for our situation—and for starting our whole Hawaiian misadventure in the first place. So while my mom, my sisters and I would all be returning to Chicago, my father would be staying behind. They would not send him a ticket or offer him a place to stay. And my parents' marriage was over, just like that.

I have to admit, besides the Dad-factor, I wasn't exactly unhappy with this turn of events. This was an opportunity to put everything that happened in Hawaii behind me—the visits from the police, the lunch tokens, my brush with crime…the whole painful, humiliating ordeal. Chicago would be a fresh start—for me and four-fifths of my family. I couldn't wait to get there and begin my new, improved life.

At least, I assumed it would be new and improved…

We moved to a suburb of Chicago called Downer's Grove, where I would enter my third 9th grade class—I'd already started high school at one school in Hawaii and moved to a second school that year. But in my mind, at least, this was it—I was finally going to make some new friends and forge a new identity in a place where nobody knew about the police coming to my house or my criminal past. Where people might think I was…here's that word again… "normal."

Unfortunately, all those new friendships and my new identity would have to wait a little longer. Because before the school year was even underway for me, I was back at home—with mono. Mono is what it is called for short. Its actual name is mononucleosis. Mono may begin slowly with fatigue, a general ill feeling, headache, and sore throat. The sore throat slowly gets worse. Your tonsils become swollen and develop a whitish-yellow covering. The lymph nodes in the neck are frequently swollen and painful (thank you Webster's dictionary).

You may have heard mono called "the kissing disease." Well, I am here to dispel that rumor once and for all. I had definitely never kissed anyone—I hadn't even had time to meet anyone yet. And instead of spending my 9th grade year forging those meaningful friendships I'd been looking forward to (and maybe even doing some kissing), I spent the first part of it in bed, and even in the hospital.

Of course, I did get better—if I hadn't, you'd be reading the sad story of some poor kid who died of mono in the 9th grade. As it was, I just had to go back to school and make up the mountain of missed work that was waiting for me. Which was not a lot of fun, and didn't exactly lend itself to a sterling school record. But academics had never really been my strong point.

At this point, I was more concerned about my next challenge—finding a place to fit in.

I was now in a position to start my new life—but where was I going to begin? Hawaii hadn't worked out very well for me. This time, I wanted to find a connection with something or someone beyond my dysfunctional family.

My grandfather, who had been an athlete back in the day, pushed me to get involved in sports. He didn't see me going too far in school—he assumed I'd just go to trade school some day since I wasn't exactly an academic standout. But I think he was also getting tired of me just sitting around the house. So he told me about the school diving team, and after spending years surrounded by water in Hawaii, it felt like the most natural place in the world for me. One of the things I did have was guts. So how hard could this be?

I made the team and finally, finally found some kids to hang out with. Things were starting to look up.

Which brings me to the title of this chapter…

Hawaii and Chicago, as you probably already know, are completely different when it comes to climate. You might think that's obvious to anybody—climate is why people leave places like Chicago to go on vacation in Hawaii in the first place! But to a young teenage boy… well, nothing is exactly obvious. If you were ever a teenage boy—or even if you've ever *known* a teenage boy—you know what I mean.

Sometimes, even the most obvious messages don't quite make it through the foggy, confused mess known as the teenage boy's brain.

So this one particular day, it was Christmas break in Chicago... and it was *cold*. I'm talking well below freezing. But even though there was no school, we still had diving practice—and the indoor heated pool where I had diving practice was nice and warm. That was part of the reason I liked the diving team so much. It was pretty cool floating in the warm water and looking at snow outside the window—especially to a kid from Hawaii!

So on this particular day, when diving practice ended, there was no school bus and my mom was at work, so I took my usual shower, dried off with a towel, got dressed and started walking home.

Which turned out to be...not the smartest thing I've ever done...

I wasn't even halfway home when I noticed my head felt kind of funny. And not funny ha-ha, funny strange—and painful! I reached up to touch my hair...

And felt a solid block of ice, or frozen spaghetti.

Yes—my hair had frozen solid.

So—here is a brief lesson for those of you who might go swimming, or even just shower, in Chicago or Minnesota or Wisconsin or any of America's chillier states from November through April...

Before you go outside, you MUST dry your hair.

Luckily (or should I say, "Oh, thank heaven!") there was a 7-11 on my way home. I ducked inside and started hopping around like a crazy person, trying to warm up and waiting for the block of ice formerly known as my hair to start melting.

The clerk behind the counter saw me and shot me a look—was he suspicious? Was my criminal past that obvious? But once I smiled at him and patted my frozen head, he knew everything he needed to know about me. He laughed hysterically. I was harmless—at least to him! Because I was a Teenage Boy.

So the clerk went back to whatever he was doing and I continued to await the Big Thaw. I didn't have to wait long. Soon, water began dripping along my scalp and down my face, down my back and underneath my coat, soaking every part of my already frozen body.

Once the last of the ice was gone, I made a mad dash for home. And since I was soaking wet, by the time I ran in the front door, my hair *and* my clothes were starting to freeze!

My grandmother hit the roof when she saw me, wet, icy and shivering. It had only been a month or two since I'd finally gotten over mono. She was convinced I'd get sick again.

But I didn't get sick. For once in my young life, I actually caught a break. Maybe things were starting to look up for me at last.

Well…not quite.

I'd been through the ulcers at ten and the mono at 14 — but my body still wasn't quite finished messing with me.

It started when some of the other kids on the dive team started making comments about my back. Since we were all in bathing suits all the time, our bodies were completely on display, and since we were teenage boys, any anomaly was duly noted. Of course, I had no idea what they were talking about since my back was behind me. I couldn't see exactly what this weird thing was. But I could feel and see in a mirror how my back was bulging out on the lower area on my left side. There was a hump to the left of where my spinal cord should be.

When I mentioned this to my mother, she knew exactly what I was talking about. Apparently, I had been given a scoliosis test back in the sixth grade — a test which came back positive. Meaning that I had scoliosis. Whatever that was.

I guess back in 6th grade it wasn't that big a deal — I spent plenty of time with my shirt off in Hawaii and no one said a thing. But as I entered adolescence, the scoliosis started doing its thing. My spine was curving the wrong way. And according to the experts, it would get worse and worse until we did something about it.

But for now, at least, I was safe. There were no trips to the doctor and no treatment plans…yet. So I kept going to diving practice, showing off my weird spine like a double-jointed elbow, or webbed toes. I may have been "The Kid with the Wacked-Out Spine," but at least I belonged somewhere. Which was all I really ever wanted.

Then, at Christmas, I received a gift that would ultimately change my life.

No, it wasn't a Luke Skywalker action figure.

It was much, much bigger than that...

My family didn't have a lot of traditions, but we did manage to get to church twice a year — for Christmas and Easter. And even though we were in a new city, this Christmas would be no exception. So on Christmas Eve, I found myself at a Methodist church about a block away from my grandparents' house.

I'd like to say something about the service that night made me feel closer to God, or helped me to know Jesus, or some other major, life changing epiphany.

Don't worry, that comes later...but not here.

At this point in my life, I was just looking for *someplace* to belong and something to do. I hadn't been in Chicago long, I'd missed months of getting-to-know-people time sitting home with mono, and I was determined that with that behind me, I was going to fit in somewhere. So when the youth pastor spotted me with my mom and sisters and approached us after the service, I saw my ticket to a new life.

We must have looked pathetic to the youth pastor — this single mother and three kids he'd never seen before showing up for the first time ever on Christmas Eve. He told my mom about the church youth group and invited me to join. Even better, he told me about something called a "lock-in" that was coming up, where all the youth group kids would stay overnight at the church.

I was in.

Looking back, I don't remember much about the lock-in itself. It wasn't the greatest night of my life or anything, but it was fun. The kids involved weren't what I would describe today as "Godly" — they chewed tobacco and used "colorful" language — but, having grown up in my not-quite-normal household, so did I.

And even though this was a church group, the kids didn't seem any more interested in God or Jesus than I was at the time. However, since some of my diving team friends were also in the youth group, and since it was the first time I really felt like I belonged somewhere, committing to this new "family" was pretty much a no-brainer.

And it would lead me to the place where I *would* ultimately change my life forever. Which is coming up…I promise.

It happened the summer after I finished 9th grade.

Through my youth group, I learned about a church camp that was being held up in Wisconsin. Silver Birch Ranch. To me—and remember, we're talking about a kid from Hawaii—this was *really* Paradise. Nestled in the hills on a lake in Wisconsin, surrounded by evergreen trees. There was no better place to just sit quietly and learn about God. Plus, a two-week excursion to a camp in Wisconsin sounded like Paradise for another, very simple reason…

It was two weeks away from home!

No mom, no sisters, no grandparents. Just me somewhere out in the wilderness, swimming, horseback riding, toasting marshmallows and just hanging out with a whole bunch of kids my own age. Amazingly, my mom agreed to let me go off on this wonderful kid vacation, and The Two Weeks That Changed My Life Forever officially began.

The first thing is, that I felt comfortable enough to let go of my security blanket; yes, I said security blanket. I sucked my thumb and required it up till this point in my life. I tried to quit, but things were so crazy for me, this was something that helped me cope. Right before my trip, I felt inside it was time to give this up, and take the next step, and so I quit, cold turkey, never to suck my thumb again.

The first week of camp really was like a vacation—and for me, it was certainly closer to a vacation than anything I'd experienced with my family. We'd never had the money for summer camps or trips to other, exotic places since I was very young…and when you're already in Hawaii, the idea of going away on vacation kind of seems silly. Not that it wouldn't have been nice…

But there was more going on at this Paradise in Wisconsin than the typical hikes and bonfires you might associate with sleep-away camp. Yes, there was plenty of fun and friendship — I met more new kids there than I ever had in my life! But this church camp was different than my youth group. There were daily Bible studies — the kind that I had never really experienced before. The kind that made me yearn for something more…something deeper than just a place to belong and people to hang out with.

I saw it in some of my fellow campers. They were so happy and so focused, and seemed untroubled by the dumb, day-to-day stuff that always threw me for a loop. And there seemed to be a reason behind their very un-teenaged-boy-like level of inner peace.

These kids talked openly about their "relationship with Christ," and how they were "saved," which meant that when their life on earth was over, they really would be going to Paradise…and it wouldn't be in Wisconsin. Or Hawaii.

These kids were just ordinary teenagers like me — but had something bigger in their lives. They had found purpose and meaning, where I had just been struggling to get along.

And suddenly I knew — I was going to have what they had. I was going to learn to have my own relationship with God and with Christ.

I was going to become a true Christian.

And then…I got a phone call from home!

At some point about halfway through my stint at camp, I got a call from my mother. Not a big deal, right? I'd never been to camp before, so I just assumed a Phone Call From Mom was part of the routine.

But it would soon become pretty obvious that this particular phone call wasn't a part of any routine — unless you count the routine known as Arthur Greeno's Crazy Life.

When I got on the phone, I was pretty much bursting with excitement. I was so excited to tell my mom about all my adventures, the words pretty much started pouring out of me. But I noticed my mom wasn't exactly engaged in the conversation.

Her voice sounded funny, and she seemed awkward, like she was trying to tell me something but just couldn't get the words out.

Have you ever seen a balloon deflate right in front of you? That was me.

With me no longer babbling like a wildman, my mom collected herself and carefully told me the reason for her phone call...

We were moving. To Tulsa, Oklahoma.

And they would be leaving first thing in the morning.

My head was spinning. What did this mean? The information was flying fast and furious. I'd remain at camp for the second week. I'd catch a Greyhound bus to Tulsa when I got back to Chicago. Tulsa was in Oklahoma. No, I would not have time to say goodbye to my friends. No, my grandparents would not be coming.

She loved me and she'd see me in a week. In a totally new city where I had never been before.

I hung up the phone and just sat there in the counselor's office. Life as I had known it was over. Yet again.

As you might imagine, I don't really remember much about my second week of camp. I'm sure there were campfires and chapel and horseback rides...but all I could think about was what was going to happen at the end of the week. Everything I'd managed to build in Downer's Grove was over. I was leaving my friends, my diving team and my church — three things that probably meant more to me than anything else in the world. But even beyond that, there were logistical issues. What if I got on the wrong bus or ended up in the wrong place? Where exactly was Tulsa, anyway?

And what was waiting for me on the other end of that bus ride?

I was about to find out.

What you want your future to look like is YOUR choice.

No one else's.

You will never have a tree if you don't first purchase a seed to plant – and YES it will take some time.

Choose and Move.

Make a choice and take action.

CHAPTER 4
ON THE ROAD AGAIN

If you start today to do the right thing, you are already a success even if it doesn't show yet.

— John C. Maxwell

You never know where you'll be when you find God speaking to you. Maybe you'll be in church, and the pastor's words will suddenly make sense to you on a level you've never felt before.

Maybe you'll be watching waves crash on a secluded beach and suddenly realize the scope of God's majesty.

Or maybe, like me, you'll be sitting on a bus.

A Greyhound bus.

After that fateful phone call from my mother, the last week of camp passed in a blur, and soon I was on the bus headed back to Chicago. But I wouldn't be going back to my grandparents' house, or to Downer's Grove, or to anyplace else in Chicagoland that was even remotely familiar.

Instead, I immediately boarded a Greyhound bus—the right one, thankfully—and began the long trip to my new home in a place called Tulsa.

Which, as I now understood it, was in Oklahoma.

So there I was, all of fifteen years old, still dressed in my stinky summer camp clothes, dragging all my worldly possessions (okay, maybe just the clothes) off one bus and onto another, headed for a completely strange destination. I just hoped the sign on top that read "Tulsa" was telling the truth. Because honestly, it was like I was making the trip on faith. Maybe this was all some elaborate plot by my mother to get rid of me! Maybe she wouldn't even be there when I got off the bus.

Of course, to make it to Tulsa to find out, I would first have to survive actually being *on* the bus.

I don't know how familiar you are with cross-country bus travel, but let me just say that in a general sense—and this does not mean that there aren't plenty of perfectly lovely people who ride buses all across the U.S.A.—but in a general sense, bus passengers, and buses in general, can be pretty scary.

First off, there's the smell.

If you can't imagine anything smellier than a 15–year-old boy returning from summer camp, clearly you have missed out on The Bus Experience. I don't know if drinking alcohol is legal on buses, but the first aroma that hit me was the unmistakable perfume of stale beer—as if a fraternity party had been held on this very bus the night before.

Combine this with the lingering scent of about sixty thousand old cigarettes, and you get that unique and unforgettable fragrance known as "Eau Du Greyhound."

But forget the smell—what really had me spooked were the other passengers. At 15, I was not long out of the "don't talk to strangers" phase, and I'd definitely never seen an assortment of strangers quite like this one. It was like I had wandered onto the Island of Lost Souls, each person scarier than the one before.

This made choosing a seat kind of a challenge. Clearly I was not going to plop myself down anywhere near the disheveled guy having a heated argument…with himself. Ditto for the old lady with the bright red lipstick who looked ready to pour her life story out to the first young man who asked. Actually, I was spooked by just about everyone—anyone who looked at me too long, or the wrong way, or avoided meeting my gaze.

Which basically included everyone on the bus.

I decided that the safest spot was most likely near the driver, so I took a seat as close to the front as I could. Hopefully that way, I would be far from any beer drinking, cigarette smoking or arguments with schizophrenics. If anything bad were to happen, I imagined he would stop it.

Looking back, I realize that may have been wishful thinking. But at the time, it was enough to get me into a seat without having a nervous breakdown!

So, my seat selected and my fears as calm as they were going to be, I settled in for the long trip "home."

Wherever that was.

Now according to Mapquest, Tulsa is a breezy 695.83 miles from Chicago—a simple 10 hour and 56 minute drive! Unfortunately, those figures don't take into account the eight hundred and seventy six stops (or at least it felt that way!) my bus would make along the way. Plus Mapquest was not invented yet.

To this day, I don't know exactly how long I was on that bus. But if my memory is correct, the trip took 16 days.

Okay, not really. But it was LONG.

So what does a 15-year-old kid do to pass the time during a seemingly-endless bus ride to a new life he didn't ask for? This was a long time before everyone had cell phones to play with, or even portable video games.

I decided, right then and there, to turn that negative into a positive. I was getting an all-new life—which meant I had a new opportunity to make sure it was a good one. So this time, I was going to do it right. I was going to try harder in school, so that I could eventually get to college. I was going to make real friends. I was going to stop hanging around with the "wrong crowd" and focus on my future.

My experience at camp really had been life changing—because it showed me exactly what had been missing from my life. Being away from the influence of the craziness of my family was powerful enough. But being surrounded by people who lived their lives in a completely different way really opened my eyes.

I witnessed every day what Christ had brought into my fellow campers' lives—and I knew in my soul that He was the answer that

I had been looking for all those years. I wasn't just looking for people to hang out with and stuff to do. I was looking for my purpose. And I found it in Jesus.

So I turned that bus to Tulsa into a sort of Bible School on Wheels. I spent hours pouring over the Bible I had read at camp, immersing myself in the Gospels and their message of hope. And I felt hopeful about my own future. There would be no more hanging out with troublemakers. There would be no more excuses about school. I would listen only to Christian music from then on. I would live the life of a committed Christian, expose myself to only the best, and trust that God would take care of the rest.

It was an amazing feeling. Even though I was headed toward a completely uncertain future, I felt more joyful than I ever had before. After so many years of struggling on my own, fighting to cope with the craziness of my family life, I had turned that massive burden over to God.

And the peace I felt inside knowing the burden was no longer on me — not that it had ever *really* been on me in the first place — was just incredible.

When I finally got off the bus in Tulsa, I was filled with so much hope and promise that when I stepped off into the blazing hot summer sun and couldn't see my mother, it didn't matter to me. I knew it was going to be all right.

But my mother *was* there to greet me and take me home. She hugged me and it felt warm and real — like the first day of the rest of my life.

When I got to my new room, one of the first things I did was get on my knees and ask Jesus into my life, starting a long-lasting personal relationship with him. I found a Christian radio station and decided that is what I would be listening to from now on. Little did I know there were at least three Christian stations in town, and I chose the one with OLD gospel music. Needless to say I suffered for Christ for quite a while before learning about the other stations.

However, if you're expecting this to be the part of the book where I suddenly get to live happily ever after...well, not quite.

Yes, I made a commitment to changing my own heart and my own soul. But I was still a kid. My *circumstances* were still basically beyond my control.

There was still my mom to deal with. With my dad long out of the picture (although my parents weren't actually legally divorced), she started dating — which meant in addition to my mom, my sisters and me, there were occasionally strange, adult men in my house. And, just like most teenage boys who suddenly find a new, grown man on their turf, I didn't like it.

So I started answering the door naked (ok, I didn't, but I thought about it).

But beyond that, my mom was still...well...my mom. She was a sweet, funny and creative person, but making a living had never been her strong suit (especially with the amount of money she spent on alcohol and cigarettes every day). And now, without my grandparents paying the bills for her, the pressure was back on my mom to keep the lights on and food on the table.

Which meant that sometimes, those lights would go off when a bill didn't get paid.

Or the water would be shut off when my mom was between jobs.

There wasn't much I could do about the first problem. But as for the second...I actually found a solution.

I was home one day and happened to see the town water truck pull up outside of our house. I watched from the window as the guy walked onto our property, turned a valve, then walked back to his truck, got in and left.

I was pretty sure I knew what I had just witnessed...so I went to the sink to check, and — jackpot! He had shut our water off. And I now knew the secret to turning it back on!

So once the truck drove away, I walked outside to the same valve I saw him turn and turned it the other way. And, just as I had hoped, we had water again.

Now, given my recent conversion and commitment to living a decent, Christian life, you might be wondering how I can possibly justify this sort of behavior. I had accepted Christ! I had pledged to turn over a new leaf! What gives?

I want to make this very clear—I felt absolutely no guilt at the time. And I still don't today.

First of all, taking that water wasn't exactly *stealing*—nothing like my Luke Skywalker escapade of a few years before—since the meter added up every gallon we used (whether we were supposed to be using it or not) and it all showed up on the bill.

But it was more than that. At the age of 15, I was taking what control I could of one of the few situations in my crazy life that I could actually do something about. I was helping to take care of my family. I was stepping up and being "the man" that our houseful of women desperately needed.

Plus, I was careful not to abuse the privilege my secret knowledge provided. So no, I wasn't belting out all my favorite Christian music hits during 30-minute showers, or luxuriating for hours in a bubble bath. I would wait until we really needed the water, then I would turn it on, go through the house and flush the toilets (very important to keep them from smelling bad!), grab a shower, and turn it back off again.

If I were in the same situation now, I'd do it again.

Although, I'd be a lot more likely to pay my water bill in the first place.

Beyond that one little bending of the rules, I really had changed my approach to life. Every day, I went to school, came home, and did my homework in front of the TV. I listened to Christian music. I read the Bible. My focus was no longer on making friends and finding "stuff to do." It was on doing what I *needed* to do to make sure I was on the right track, and headed toward the kind of life I wanted to live.

And of course, the minute I stopped trying so hard, friends wound up finding me anyway. I joined the soccer team –I started playing in 2nd grade and have always loved it—and wound up getting friendly with my coach's son and his family. They belonged to a different church than any I had experienced before—the Assemblies of God.

Since there was no longer a church within walking distance of my house, and since it was very important to me to continue to go to church and grow in my faith, I got a ride with my new friend and his family every week.

For quite a while I tried to get my mom out of bed to take me to church on Sunday mornings, but she would drink on Friday nights, all day Saturdays till way late, and usually she would go to a bar late Saturday night. Getting her up early Sunday was a piece of work. So at first I would ride with anyone, to any church. Things stabilized when the Harmon family started allowing me to join them (they would also allow me to use their mower since we never had one, and when the grass was…say 12 inches high I would mow it, and return the mower).

I definitely appreciated this family taking me under their wing, and I still do. They helped put me in front of Godly people. Despite my recent commitment to changing my life and my outlook, I was still pretty rough around the edges. It wasn't that I was a "bad kid," it was just that I never learned from my parents or anyone else that phrases like "son of a b****" and words like "hell" aren't regarded as "polite conversation" — and certainly not appropriate at school or in church!

Sometimes when I would speak, people's mouths would just fall open, or they'd give me dirty looks. That is always a good clue what you said was not appropriate. Okay, actually that still happens today, but not because of my potty mouth, thank you!

Anyway, slowly but surely, I started to train myself. I learned to operate in "polite society."

My friend and I also joined the Royal Rangers, which was like the Boy Scouts, but specifically for Christian boys. I loved it. I felt special, like I was a part of something great—and it helped me to stay focused on my growing faith and my relationship with Christ, which was becoming more important every day.

That faith is what really gave me the strength and the confidence to approach life in a new way. With God on my side, I could take on responsibility for what happened to me in my life. I didn't do my homework because my mom nagged me to; I did it because I made it a priority. I didn't learn to watch my language because anyone told me to, I did it because I was teaching myself how to live the life a person dedicated to Christ should live.

I was making progress, and it felt good.

But I was also learning that creating the kind of life I wanted really was up to me. Whatever my family did or did not provide me with, I had the power to make choices. I could choose to try, or to slack off. To learn, or to cut myself off. To succeed, or to fail.

With God's help, I chose success.

At one point when my family lived in Hawaii, we had gone through an Experiential Training Course on Self Development. The results worked for a little while, but were short lived. Things at the house changed for a short time, but then the Chaos came back. I was very young and my need for attention was running pretty rampant at that time. I don't remember much about that weekend, but what I do remember is this: Personal Accountability, that I am the one responsible. It's my fault. No matter what happens in life, it's my fault... good or bad. If I am able to succeed in life it will be because of me. If I end up not succeeding, it will also be my fault. This concept did not sink in right away, but about the time I really needed it, it would.

CHAPTER 5
SETTLING IN

The difference between winners and losers is that winners do things losers don't want to do.

— Phillip C. McGraw

B y the end of my first year in Tulsa, a new, improved Arthur Greeno had emerged. I had stayed true to the promises I made to myself and to God on that endless bus ride the summer before, when I had never heard of Tulsa and had no idea what my new life was going to bring. Sitting there on that bus, I decided that I was going to take responsibility for my life. I set standards for myself — and over the months that followed, I worked hard to meet those standards.

And my life actually changed!

It was an incredible feeling. I was losing that tendency to blame my parents or my circumstances for things that went wrong for me — especially since, now that I was working harder, less things seemed to be going wrong for me. I had taken responsibility for my own future, and for the first time, things had started going my way.

Of course, when you're 15 years old with no money, there's still a limit to what you can control…

This became clear as the school year drew to a close. I really, really wanted to go back to the Silver Birch Ranch in Wisconsin where the whole "life changing thing" had started the summer before.

But without any money to pay for camp, that was pretty much impossible, right?

Where does a 15-year-old kid come up with the money for summer camp? My mom didn't have it. I wasn't going to beg for it. And it's not like there was a Summer Camp Fairy who would leave a golden ticket under my pillow one night...

I could have given up. I wanted to be back there so bad! It was really the only place I felt at peace, where my surroundings weren't overwhelming me.

I decided that I would do whatever it took to go back (within the law). I prayed God would open a door for me, and he did, through an idea...

I wondered, what would happen if I called the camp and explained my situation and offered to work to pay my way? The worst they could say was no, right? So I took a deep breath, called the camp organizers and told them my story—I explained how much I wanted to be there, and offered to do just about anything they needed to earn the chance to go back.

And guess what?

The camp organizers were all for it! As long as I did maintenance, dishes and helped out around the camp, I could stay there for the entire summer.

Yes, you heard that right. Not just two weeks. The entire summer.

My head was spinning. I'd just been given the most incredible gift of my young life. But there was one rather major complication left...

How was I going to afford a bus ticket to Wisconsin?

At 15, I was still too young for a "real" job—and even if I could find one, there wasn't enough time to earn the kind of cash I needed to get all the way to Wisconsin and back, my mom certainly had no money, and my dad was still in Hawaii dealing with other debt.

I wracked my brain for a solution. There had to be one—I'd already come this far! I couldn't let this opportunity pass me by...

Then I learned that the Royal Rangers, the Christian scout organization I belonged to, would be holding a Bowl-a-Thon in a few weeks—and the person who raised the most money for charity would get a gift certificate to the Woodland Hills Mall in Tulsa.

Bingo.

If they'd shell out money for a shopping spree at a mall, surely they'd help a dedicated young man get to camp for the summer. It was, after all, a Christian camp, and the Royal Rangers was a Christian organization. Sounds like a no-brainer to me...

So, I took another in a series of deep breaths and presented my very logical case to the Bowl-a-Thon organizers. And while they weren't quite as understanding and accommodating as the camp people, they did agree that if I won, they would, in fact, pay my bus fare. (I wonder what they were thinking. This new kid coming in, and negotiating on if he wins?)

The trick was, I had to win.

And honestly, what were the chances of *that* happening?

They didn't know the New, Improved Arthur Greeno (actually most of them did not know the Old Arthur Greeno either). But they were about to meet him.

I was going to do everything I could to make my dream come true. In order for this to happen, I determined that I needed two things. I needed to bowl decently...but more importantly, I needed sponsors.

The way a bowl-a-thon works is, you get as many people as you can to sponsor you, promising to donate a certain amount of money to the charity or organization based on how many points you score. So even if you don't score a lot of points, if you have enough sponsors, you can still win the big prize. That, I realized, was my easiest path to victory.

So I hit up everyone I could find. Friends and their parents, their neighbors, my neighbors, complete strangers...no one was safe from my pleas. And when I had completely exhausted the neighborhoods of everyone I knew, I went to local malls and stores and asked every single person who walked by to sponsor me.

And a lot of them did. Turns out those skills I honed back in Hawaii looking for friends door-to-door came in handy!

When I turned my paperwork in, the organizers' mouths fell open as they thumbed through page after page after page of sponsors. But I was way ahead of them. I had moved on to Phase 2—the bowling phase.

I had some bowling experience from my days in Hawaii. But I didn't want to get fancy. I came up with a very simple plan. Don't worry about technique, or looking cool, or anything except this: get the ball down to the end of the lane. The rest would take care of itself.

And it did.

I won the contest.

The organizers were true to their word and paid for my bus ticket. I spent my entire summer at camp. And it was just as amazing as I had expected it would be. I worked hard, made friends and participated in all kinds of activities. In fact, it was even better than I had expected, because knowing that I was earning my stay there felt good. It made me feel powerful to see that I really could help shape my own destiny—that if I wanted something badly enough and worked hard enough, I could actually get it.

Those lessons stuck with me for the rest of my life.

I learned: Sometimes the only solution is the one that's not easy. "Think outside the box" for the solution if it is not right in your face.

Sometimes it will require some sacrifice (for me it was time).

I also learned that luck favors the prepared.

Another thing that stuck with me from that summer was the fact that I needed to find a new church. When I mentioned to one of the Elders at camp that I had been going to the Assemblies of God church in Tulsa, he suggested that might not be the right place for me. I had to agree—the church hadn't been a perfect fit (not that there is anything wrong with the church, I just was looking for something a little different). So, I agreed that when I got home, I would look for a non-denominational church. That's what the camp was, and I wanted that same sense of belonging at home.

But before I could find my new church, I had one more complication to deal with in my already-complicated life. My junior year was about to become the year of…the Brace.

While my life had been getting better, that scoliosis that I mentioned a while back had been getting worse. My mother took me to the doctor before school started, and he decided that the curvature in my spine needed to be dealt with ASAP. That meant I would need to wear a metal brace for the next two years—which were also my last two years of high school...

You've gotta be kidding.

After everything I'd been through, after all the hard work I'd put in, *this happened?* What girl would ever consider going out with me? It would be like dating the tin man. How was I supposed to enjoy my last high school years?

It was all too much. Sitting there in the doctor's office, I started to cry. Not the feel-sorry-for-yourself kind, but actually more like the really, really mad kind. The kind where the tears would stream off your face before it hits your chin kind. I was MAD! Partially at God. It was like, "Hey! I am doing what I can, why can't I get a break!?"

Not that it made a difference. My spine was curving into an "S," which was not the proper shape for a spine. And it would only get worse. So I was fitted for what's called a Milwaukee Brace, a contraption that kind of resembles a medieval torture device. It extended from my pelvis all the way up to my chin, and was made up of steel rods, straps to hold it in place, and latches to keep the scoliosis from getting worse.

And yes, it was every bit as uncomfortable as it sounds.

Sitting in a car was almost impossible—the seat pushed up on the brace until it would push up on my chin. I couldn't even ride in certain cars—if they were too small, they couldn't accommodate me. At school, sitting at my desk was also a challenge—I had to sit on the very edge of my seat with my legs tucked under the seat just to fit under the desk. Some desks had small openings that would tear my shirts getting in and out.

Of course, physical discomfort was only the tip of this particular iceberg. Chances are, if you're reading this, you went to high school. In which case, I don't need to tell you how cruel kids can be. And the sight of me clanging through the halls in my metal cage...well, I guess I was too tempting a target to ignore. They called me R2D2... they called me Robo-Boy...it was not a lot of fun. And certainly not

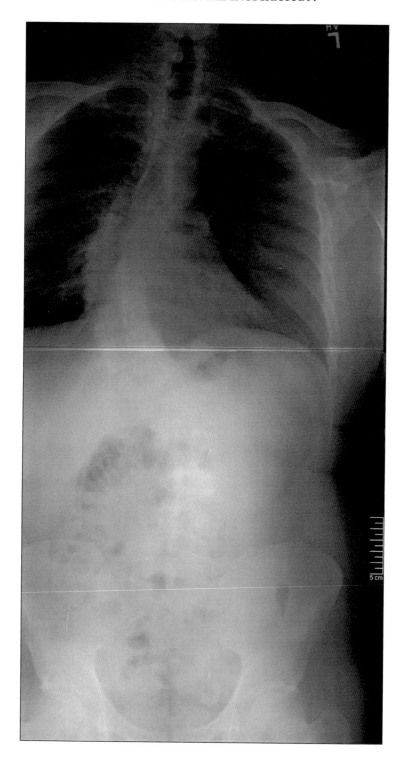

the junior year I had envisioned for myself.

But something inside me wouldn't let me fall apart this time. I had come so far—I had survived my mother's drinking, my parents' fighting and moves all over the country. I had found God, improved my grades and turned my life around. Maybe the old me would have given up and decided it was all too hard. But now I understood. I knew I had a choice. And I chose to live my life the best way I could.

Even today, I still have some physical limitations. I have endured many hours of back pain as my body and I wrestle to figure out just what those limitations are. Looking back, if I had to do it over again, and we had the means, I would have treated my scoliosis with surgery. Those muscles still grew, and grew wrapped around the bone, which makes certain things really painful, even today. However, I have adapted, and today I can almost always tell when I am about to have a "muscle issue"—so I go and rest so I can fight another day.

Back then, living my best life started with keeping the promise I made at camp and looking for a non-denominational church. When I found the one that felt right to me, it clearly happened for a reason. Because along with my new church came a bonus—a person who would become one of my closest friends for the rest of my life.

When I asked Darrell Cleaver if his parents would mind giving me a ride to church with them, I had no idea of the impact that simple request would have on my life. Soon, I was spending every weekend with the Cleavers—I'd head over to their house after school on Friday, and I'd stay with them until they dropped me off at home after church on Sunday night. They became like my second family— his parents even set up a bunk bed for me. And Darrell became more than a friend—he was like the brother I never had. He accepted me for who I was, crazy family and metal brace and all. And that unconditional support and acceptance made those months with the brace much, much easier.

The actress Marlene Dietrich once said, "It is the friends you can call up at 4am that matter." That's the thing about true friends. They stick with you no matter what. When you have burdens, they share them with you. They bring light into your world. Darrell did that for me. (Darrell, I want my picture of Batman back!)

Grace Church in Tulsa was also a sanctuary — a place where my brace and my family background didn't matter either. I joined the youth group, and my circle of friends grew to include two more guys, Mark Collier and Mike Tedford — two guys who didn't need a back brace to be dorks. They came by it naturally (he, he).

Thanks to them, my junior year — and those months of wearing a back brace for 23 hours a day — passed by without any more tears or major incidents. Not to give you the impression everything was perfect — it wasn't. I still had to deal with my home situation with my mom, my missing my dad, and our constant money issues — not to mention the fact that my upper torso had the flexibility of Frankenstein. But I had direction, and purpose. I stayed on track and on target. And eventually, the strangest thing began to happen...

I started to get popular in the youth group.

Of course, that might have had something to do with the gorilla mask.

It's like this. Walking around in a back brace, you tend to get a lot of stares from people. So I decided that if people were going to stare at me, I might as well have a little fun with them. Enter...the gorilla mask.

We were at a costume shop getting practical joke stuff and they had this goofy latex gorilla mask on sale. I just could not pass it up.

I'd put it on, and suddenly when people stared at me, they stared because they were entertained, or surprised, or even annoyed. It didn't matter, as long as they were NOT staring because they felt sorry for the poor kid in a back brace.

I wore the mask when I wore the brace — and even when I didn't. People's reactions were just priceless. It was so much fun to wear it out and see what would happen next.

Imagine being at a concert, minding your own business and sort of gazing around the crowd — and spotting what looks like a gorilla rocking along with the music. Come on...you'd have to laugh...

unless you're easily fooled and very, very afraid of gorillas. In which case you might run.

Whenever there was a concert or event, I'd bring out my mask… and attend as Gorilla Boy. And I quickly discovered that it wasn't just ordinary Joes and Janes who noticed the gorilla in their midst. If there were video cameras around covering the event, chances were good they'd grab a shot of my friends and me. Pretty soon we were popping up in music videos and pictures all over. We were local celebrities…sort of.

And that, although I didn't realize it at the time, was the start of another big thing in my life. I learned that being goofy gets you noticed. And what was fun and kind of a novelty for a high school kid would prove to be serious business when I needed to attract attention when I got older.

One time I was getting an award for something, and I was standing in this big long line of people. I had this shirt that had a bunch of padding and was flesh colored, making it look like I was this really buff guy. So while standing in line about to go on stage I put it on. And then I pulled out my metal Viking hat with horns on it that I had bought earlier that day, and put it on.

The guy standing two spots up from me looked back and said, "Why are you doing that?" I responded, "A month from now, who do you think is going to be remembered: the guy in the tie, or me?" He responded, "Thanks a lot!"

But that was later. For now, I was happy enough with my newfound fame and growing popularity.

As I headed into my senior year, my brace time was cut in half — to twelve hours a day. This allowed me to run track and cross country, which was heaven after being caged for so long. I also got my first real job — at…wait for it…McDonald's.

I know, I know. Not exactly the healthy paradise known as Chick-fil-A. But Darrell and Mark both worked there, I could get a ride with them, and besides, just about every other red-blooded American kid in the '80s and '90s put in some hours at the Golden Arches.

Did I learn anything during those first heady months in the food-service industry that have helped me today? I'll just say I learned a lot...about what to do, and some stuff about what *not* to do! Remember, I was a teenage boy and I loved to act crazy. So if you happened to consume any food that I came in contact with back then, I sincerely apologize...

And if you happen to work for me now and are getting any bright ideas, I have one word for you.

Don't. Anything you're thinking of, I have either done, or seen done!

Between the job, the gorilla mask and the popularity, senior year was when it all came together for me. My father even moved down to Tulsa to be with us so he could see me graduate, which meant a lot to me. And with my unusual family complete in its own way, another, final piece of the puzzle finally fell into place.

Suddenly, I was starting to get popular around the youth group, and also with girls.

Yes, at long last, women were noticing me. Who knew a back brace and a gorilla mask were surefire ways to pick up chicks? Maybe on their own, not so much, but something about my self-deprecating brand of self-confidence had appeal.

I started dating — first with the guys, and later on my own. Oops, wait, its not how it sounds. I mean I would go out on double dates with my friends, then later on my own. I think I went out with about six girls in my youth group in just a few months. It was all innocent, I promise!

But there was one very cute girl who was a few years younger than me who would become very important later on. She was off-limits to me — I was dating her best friend at the time and the cute girl I was admiring had some boyfriend that she was in band with. But still, there was something there... Her name was Noell. Deep down inside, she knew she wanted to marry me... Hey! It's my book; it's how I remember it! Don't believe a word Noell tells you.

CHAPTER 6
HOW TO GO TO COLLEGE WITH ABSOLUTELY NO MONEY

Success is connected with action. Successful people keep moving. They make mistakes, but they don't stop.

-Arthur Greeno

With high school behind me, it was time for the next stage of the adventure otherwise known as my life. That meant college.

College wasn't exactly the expected next step for a kid in my family. Even though my father, as a math professor, was obviously an educated person, neither of my parents worried all that much (or, to be honest, at all!) about how I was doing in school. Nobody thought of me as any sort of great intellectual. My grandfather, who was really the only person in my family to talk about my future at all, had advised me back in 9th grade to plan for trade school—because I was not (in his opinion) smart enough for college.

But that wasn't part of *my* plan, or, for that matter, God's plan. I would go to college.

I already had a school in mind—Oral Roberts University. Oral Roberts is a Christian College, and to be honest, I never really considered a different school—since dedicating my life to Christ, things had completely turned around for me and I knew that I was following the right path.

In fact, my career goal at the time was to become a youth pastor. My own youth pastors, Larry Engel and Greg Ball, both had a huge impact on my life. So if any youth pastors are reading this right now, and for some reason feel like you don't make a difference — YOU DO!

After everything I had been through in my crazy childhood, after all my youth pastors had done for me, I felt almost like it was a calling. With God's help — and okay, by working really hard — I turned out okay. What an amazing story to be able to share with other kids like me, who might not feel like they exactly fit in. I could picture myself helping them open up to Christ and watching as their lives changed in amazing, profound ways...

...all while wearing a gorilla mask.

You have to admit, it was a pretty good fit.

Anyway, as one of America's top Christian universities, Oral Roberts was an ideal place to prepare for a career as a youth pastor.

That and the fact that it was *right there in Tulsa* didn't hurt. And Darrell and Mike were both going there. So basically, choosing Oral Roberts was a complete no-brainer.

However, this was still my life, and in typical fashion, there were still going to be a few hurdles to clear.

First, I would have to be accepted.

This was not going to be a no-brainer, unless we're talking about *my* brain. I'm not a person who, as they say, "tests well." This was probably a lasting effect of my not-exactly-rigorous academic upbringing. I have always had trouble concentrating, and my father told me a couple of years ago that some teachers had told him I would never be able to read. So, the first time I took the ACT, I got a whopping 14.

For those of you who don't know, the ACT is one of those standardized tests like the SAT that's supposed to measure whether or not you've got the right stuff for college. Oral Roberts required a score of 18 — and while I don't remember the exact scope of the ACT scale, I do remember things were not looking good with that 14.

My GPA wasn't much help either. Yes, I worked my backside off those last three years in high school, but thanks to all those D's and F's I got back in 9th grade, I just barely squeaked in above a 3.0.

But since I was the "New, Improved Arthur Greeno," and since Oral Roberts clearly appeared to be part of God's plan for me, giving up was simply not an option.

I took the ACT again and got a 17 — and Oral Roberts accepted me…conditionally. I would be on probation and had to maintain a C average. That was good enough for me. I saw no reason why I wouldn't be able to meet their expectations. Heck, I planned to exceed them.

Having been accepted, it was now on to the next issue — how was I going to pay to attend a private university? Especially as a kid coming from a family with no money?

To be honest, I wasn't worried about that either. After getting myself to Silver Birch Ranch camp for an entire summer as a high school sophomore, I had learned to trust in God. As long as I gave it my best effort — and those three words, *my best effort*, are the key here — I knew He would take care of the rest.

"When it's all said and done, I want to stand before God and know there was nothing else I could do." That's a quote to this day I use.

Maybe that's why money never played a role when I decided what I was going to do with my life after high school. I trusted that I was following a path, and if God had a different plan for me, I figure I would have been led in another direction.

I think about that when I see or hear things about this new debate over whether the cost of college is actually worth it. Kids are graduating tens and even hundreds of thousands of dollars in debt, and some "experts" are coming out and saying that maybe college isn't the right choice for everyone.

I see it a little differently. I saw a recent study (done, apparently, by another group of "experts"), that said that people with a college degree will earn, on average, twenty thousand dollars more per year than a person with only a high school diploma. That's hundreds and hundreds of thousands of thousands of dollars over a lifetime. Do the math, and clearly a college education is worth it.

But there's so much more to it than that. A college education exposes you to the world beyond your town and your friends and your family. It gives you the tools that you need to tackle the challenges life throws at you. It may not be for everyone, but I believe that it's still right for a *lot* of people. So my unsolicited advice here is that, if college sounds right to you, do everything you can to make it happen.

I promise you, if you take the opportunity seriously, you will not be disappointed.

The way I took it seriously was by making going to Oral Roberts a goal. In order to qualify for financial aid, I had to provide tax forms from my mom and dad. Since they never officially divorced, this bumped the money the two of them made up just to the poverty level — even though they lived two totally separate lives with separate homes, bills and everything. But the powers that be didn't take this into account, so their combined income was deemed too high for everything to be taken care of. So I had to keep filling out more forms and papers to prove that I really had no way of coming up with money to pay for school.

If there was a grant or loan or scholarship that I had the *opportunity* to apply for, I did it. I looked at finding money to pay for school like it was my job, just like working at McDonald's (which at the time was still my job) — and I did anything I could to get through school, giving plasma, any odds-and-ends job. Anything.

And I would do it all over again today.

Part of the big push for me was I needed to get out of the house. It was too rough at home. Lorine moved out the second she could, the day after she graduated, and Kathleen stayed with Mom for a short time after I moved out. She got pregnant at 15 and by 17 had moved out. I would see them on Holidays, and send them cards on birthdays, but I really had to move on from that part of my life in order to achieve whatever the future held for me.

As a Christian university, Oral Roberts has a few more rules than the average institution of higher learning. There was mandatory Chapel twice a week, and I needed to take a Bible class on something like the Old Testament, the New Testament or the Holy Spirit every semester. The school had a dress code which meant I had to wear my hair cut short and dress in a shirt and tie every day, like a businessman. Beards were forbidden (although moustaches were okay!), and as you might imagine, drinking or smoking on campus was absolutely not allowed.

None of this should have been a problem for me. Maybe I needed to supplement my wardrobe, but I certainly didn't drink or smoke.

But you wouldn't know that if you happened to smell me.

My mother was a chain-smoker. If you've ever known a chain smoker, if you've ever been in a house where a chain-smoker lives, you know, it kind of has its own signature aroma. Everything—the furniture, the walls, the carpet—it all smells like smoke. What you might not know is, if you spend your entire life in a place like that, *you* start to smell like smoke too. It gets in your clothes, your hair, even your skin. It's almost like *you've* been smoked—like you're a slab of bacon or a Christmas ham.

And the smell sticks with you (or on you), even after you leave.

As a result, I was suddenly America's Most Wanted…at least in my dorm.

The RA (that's resident advisor, if you've never lived in a dorm) in charge of keeping order in my dorm was convinced that I was, in fact, hiding a smoking habit.

And he made it his personal mission to catch me in the act. One day, though, something happened that finally made him stop. Late one night, he must have thought I was in my room smoking, and using his key, decided to burst into my room to catch me in the act. Hearing his keys rattling and expecting Darrell to come in, I turned out the lights and climbed on the top bunk. I got into position, and as he walked in, I jumped on his back, screaming as high-pitched as I could. I should also mention that, like many male Americans, I slept in my underwear. Well, as soon as I realized it wasn't Darrell, I let go, laughing hysterically. He did not think it was funny. He never snuck in my room to do that again, but this guy must have thought he was the star of *CSI: Oral Roberts University*. He literally tracked me. When I left the dorm, he would follow me around outside, no doubt to get an idea of my "whereabouts." And when tailing me didn't produce any leads, he interrogated my friends to get them to confess to him that yes, Arthur Greeno was a big, smoky smoker. From Smoketown.

Except I didn't smoke.

So he never caught me.

There were other strict rules at Oral Roberts, too. Women were not allowed in the men's dorms — and vice-versa, although I didn't live in a woman's dorm so I can't be 100% sure. Maybe that's why Darrell, my good buddy turned roommate, spent hours on the phone talking to girls...and locking me out of our room. Darrell's a good friend, but he also happened to be one of those guys where you knew everything you needed to know about his love life solely by how much he was hanging around with you. When things on the romantic front picked up, he would disappear. So I would end up spending a little more time with Mike, who didn't vanish every time a pretty girl entered his life.

Freshman life at Oral Roberts basically consisted of the typical college stuff. I stayed up way too late talking and listening to music and hanging out. And, being me, I played my share of jokes and pranks. Like the time I decided to run for student office as a write-in candidate.

My very first semester there.

Yes, just because I was being a serious college student didn't mean I stopped being a goofball. And no, I had no idea that somehow, either by running for student office as a freshman, or maybe by putting up flyers in the cafeteria, I was breaking the rules. Come to think of it, I found out a lot of things were against the rules...after I broke them. And to be completely honest (I don't want to lie in my own book!), I would do it again. Not all rules are made to be broken; but sometimes breaking them can be a lot of fun.

Especially if you're really not interested in being president.

Anyway, I launched my "campaign" for student office with the help of my friends. We put up posters all over campus and plastered the name "Arthur Greeno" everywhere we could. We put table tents up in the cafeteria—we worked as a well-oiled machine, we were in and out before anyone could tell us we were not allowed to do it. We got one of those old television sets—the ones made like a piece of furniture with the screen in a sort of wooden cabinet—then removed the tube and put my picture where the screen had been. Except, instead of my picture, it was a picture of me in my gorilla mask, along with one of those cartoon bubble quotes saying something like, 'Would you trust a face like this?'

I didn't realize it at the time, but my friends and I were learning something valuable while making total fools of ourselves…or at least me. We had accidentally embarked on a crash course in good, old-fashioned marketing. After all, what is marketing except getting the name and/or image of a product or business out there to generate interest and attention? Well, I got plenty of interest and attention with my campaign.

Maybe some of it was from the wrong people, or for the wrong reasons, but it was most definitely attention!

So, the campaign season wore on until Election Day finally rolled around—and guess what happened?

I won and became the Student Body President of Oral Roberts University, and got a new car, and moved to the penthouse.

Okay…maybe not.

This is not one of those "Arthur Triumphs Over Adversity" stories. Yes, there are a lot of those in here, but this wasn't about my battling the odds to win the election or anything dramatic like that. It was just a prank that made my friends and me laugh, that I hoped would make some people laugh—and give me that moment in the spotlight, being the funny guy I so loved to be.

That said, I actually did get a fair number of votes—way too many for a candidate whose platform basically consisted of breaking rules and wearing a gorilla mask. But for me, the biggest deal was that when the votes were all tallied and the winners were announced, they came looking for me.

"They" being the winners.

And no, they didn't come after me to take me on, or challenge me over breaking the rules or anything like that. They just wanted to meet me and find out who "the guy in the gorilla mask" was!

But all my pranks weren't politically motivated. There were also… the "Dessert Wars."

"Dessert Wars" was the name of a game my friends and I would play while eating in the cafeteria. It basically consisted of destroying each other's food, mixing random ingredients, pouring juice or milk on top of someone's dessert, and making other inedible concoctions like some sort of evil Food Network chef.

Sometimes we would even make bets to see who would dare to eat our creations (I made some good cash this way). I am still trying to figure out how the live fish ended up in the desserts that one time…

What can I say? We were gross.

How gross? Well, one day, my friend Mike bought a brownie. In true Dessert Wars fashion, I reached across the table and squished his brownie in my hand, so that it became a long, cylindrical brown clump. I sat it back down on the plate and, as expected, all of our friends and other random spectators laughed.

There was no denying what that squished, brown mound looked like.

So Mike had lost his craving for a brownie…but I wasn't quite done with it yet. I wrapped the brownie in some plastic wrap and took it back to my dorm room. Then I filled up a 5-gallon bucket of water and brought that back to my room (yes, don't you keep a 5-gallon bucket around your room just in case you want to play a joke?).

I had a plan. Now I had to wait for just the right moment.

Days passed while I stalked my prey. In the bathroom. (Can you see where this is going?) And then one day, the perfect circumstances arose. The bathroom was deserted, except for one lonely soul who sat in a stall doing his business.

I rushed back to my room, grabbed my bucket and my brownie and I was off. I took up residence in the stall directly next to the poor schmuck (which, if you know anything about bathroom etiquette, is a total faux pas). Then I sat down on the toilet and began making small talk (another noted faux pas).

The Stall Dweller did not respond to my banter. But when the moment was just right, I knew I would get a response out of him yet...

I stood up, flushed the toilet and, in my most worried voice, exclaimed, "Oh no! Oh no! The toilet's overflowing! Lift your feet! What do I do? How can I make it stop?"

Stall Dweller stuttered. I could hear my friends, who had come to watch the show from the hall, snickering in the background. Then it was time. I got my 5-gallon bucket ready and poured the water underneath the stall, toward my victim. As he howled about his wet shoes, I added the *piece de resistance*. I unwrapped the smashed brownie and dropped it in the puddle.

The guy jumped up and out through the swinging door. I just stood there saying, "I don't know what happened."

"You need to clean it up!" he stammered.

I didn't move. "It's not mine, I swear, it's not mine, it just came out of the toilet, I swear it's not mine!"

Stall Dweller started gathering up his pants, looking at me as if I were Lucifer incarnate. By this time, a crowd had gathered, some knowing about the origin of the brown mound, while others...well, I could tell from their faces that they made the same assumption as the Stall Dweller. This included the chaplain, who was standing outside the door. He could see in and see what was going on, but also could see my friends sitting in the hall crying. They knew the fatal moment, because his face described in detail what happened, but this just made them laugh even harder.

Then it was time for my big moment. Pulling my inspiration directly from one of the great comedic geniuses in one of the funniest movies of all time—Bill Murray in *Caddyshack*—I picked up the mound, examined it closely, and, relishing every second of disgust from the crowd...I bit into it.

It wasn't too bad for a soggy, week-old brownie.

Stall Dweller actually started screaming and ran out the other door, leaving Mike and the crowd rolling on the hallway floor crying. He saw them and ran right to his room, not putting together why they were all there laughing. All he knew was what he saw, and what he saw was nasty.

I explained to as many people as I could where the brown stuff had come from, but it didn't matter. From that day forward, my reputation spread. I was one of the greatest pranksters on campus.

Or at least I had made a name for myself.

Mike still can't get through that story without laughing to tears.

Now, I don't want you to get the wrong idea here. It's not like I spent every minute at ORU concocting genius pranks — those were my big two. Well...there were a couple more. The Ex-Lax brownie was great, since one of my friends (the mooch) ate some (as expected) and had the runs for a week. And then there was the time I took chocolate covered cherries and filled them with Tabasco...

Still, being economically-challenged *and* on probation, I did have to spend an awful lot of my time studying. Maybe that's why, when I did pull a prank, I made sure it was a BIG one!

Work-wise, I had kept the job at McDonald's and added a work-study job so that I could handle my college expenses. And even with two jobs, I still had to give plasma to keep gas in my $200, 14-year-old Ford. It wasn't easy, but it all seemed to be working. I was staying in school and making good grades. Eventually, I wasn't even on probation anymore.

The months flew by, and soon I was looking forward to my first summer as a college student, where I'd be working alongside my friend Mike as a counselor at a Christian camp called Camp Dry Gulch.

Yes, my life was definitely starting to come together.

And then...I got the Bill.

CHAPTER 7
HOW TO STAY IN COLLEGE WITH ABSOLUTELY NO MONEY

Success doesn't come to you — you go to it, it's not by accident, but by intent.

-Arthur Greeno

At some point late in my freshmen year at Oral Roberts, I was notified that one of my grants for financial aid hadn't completely come through. What that meant, in a nutshell, was that I owed the school money. A lot of money.

At the time I found out, there wasn't much I could do about it. The end of the school year and finals and hopefully landing a summer job were all fast approaching. Between my two jobs and my occasional plasma donations, I had enough to complete the semester, but not enough to come back to ORU in the fall. But I didn't really have time to worry. Besides, God had gotten me through so far. All I had to do was keep on putting one foot in front of the other, taking things one step at a time, and giving everything I did everything I had.

I trusted that the rest would work out okay.

A summer job was key to the plan, and I was lucky to find a great one. One great thing about ORU was the fact that people were always coming to campus to recruit college students to work for their companies and organizations. Actually, that's also another great thing about college in general—it doesn't just provide you with an education and prepare you for life and your future, it also opens up a whole world of very real work opportunities right then and there.

One day in the lunchroom, Mike and I spotted a recruiter from Camp Dry Gulch who was looking for counselors for the summer session. Naturally, I was interested. My time at summer camp in Wisconsin was not only among the best times of my life; it actually gave me my life! So the idea of being able to do that for a group of kids—and being outside in the sun and the fresh air instead of stuck behind a deep fryer all summer long—sounded like the ultimate summer job (as well as great training for a future youth pastor). Mike agreed, and we both signed up.

The camp, located in Adair, Oklahoma, was modeled after an Old West town—complete with a bunch of old, western-looking houses (as you might expect in an Old West town), a main street, an outdoor pole barn chapel and a cafeteria. Through the week, I worked with the kids, but once one group would leave, we had 24 hours off, and I would hang out with my fellow counselors—many of whom went to a local school called Rhema Bible College.

The more time I spent with them, the more I started to question my future at Oral Roberts. Which, in hindsight, I realize is a completely normal thing to do. When you're 19 or 20 years old and planning the rest of your life, you're bound to question whether or not the path you're on is the right one. And suddenly, I started having doubts about mine.

Obviously, there was the matter of that money I owed. Being in debt felt very, very serious to me at the age of 19, with the ability to earn not a whole lot more than minimum wage. But I also started to question whether Oral Roberts was really the right fit for me spiritually.

I personally believe in the God that—when you're hurting—reaches around you and gives you a hug when you need it. I believe in the God who gives you a hand up, like He has given to me countless times. But some of the people in my theology classes didn't see it that way—or at least, were content spending what seemed like endless amounts of time arguing over what were, in my opinion, ridiculous things.

I didn't want to argue, that wasn't what I signed up for. You know when TV commentators talk about "pointy-headed intellectuals" who waste time debating stupid things for what seems like endless amounts of time? It was like that to some degree. They just went on and on and on until I actually got dizzy. I was not having any fun — it was ALL WORK!

The counselors I met who went to Rhema weren't interested in endless debates about the nature of God. They seemed like they were well-grounded people with their heads on straight — the kind of people who I could relate to. So there, at camp, I decided not to return to ORU. When I got home, I enrolled at Rhema instead.

Rhema certainly worked with my schedule — it was a ½ day school and let out at noon, which gave me time to work all afternoon and evening. But not everyone was happy with my new educational path. Surprisingly, my parents, who had never paid attention to my education at all, were suddenly expressing an opinion about my studies. Their verdict: Rhema wasn't a real college and not good enough for me. I should go back to ORU.

Part of me was pretty annoyed with their sudden interest in my educational path. Who were they, after not caring about how I did in school for 13 years, to weigh in with an opinion about my future?

But on the other hand (and there always is another hand, isn't there?), the fact that my parents — *my parents* — had both chosen that particular moment to get involved with my educational life had to mean something. Could they have actually been impressed by everything I had done to get to Oral Roberts? Did they think I was worthy of a real university degree? Did they think I deserved a better life?

Ultimately, my parents' objections forced me to give some more thought to the best way to prepare for my future.

And when I did, I had to consider the possibility that maybe they were right — maybe Rhema wasn't the best place for me. After all, a degree from Rhema would only put me in the position to do one thing—work in a church in some capacity. What if I didn't really want to be a youth pastor? What if God had something else in mind for me? Should I concentrate on a degree that would allow me to keep my options open?

Ultimately, I had to agree with my parents. I withdrew from Rhema and returned to Oral Roberts. Which, I imagine, is what God had in mind for me all along.

Of course, this still left the matter of the bill from the previous year. I had been making payments all summer, but I still was not caught up, and I needed to pay another $1,000 to get back in. At that point, my dad stepped in and was able to get a guaranteed government loan to pay the $1,000. This was a very big deal for my father, that he was finally able to do something to help me get through college. I was, and still am, very grateful.

Next, I needed a place to live. The good news was, Oral Roberts did not require sophomores to live on-campus *if* they were living with their parents, which meant I would no longer have to worry about the expense of room and board. The bad news—the living *with my parents* part! My mom was a sweet, loving person, but living with her was not the greatest experience. After spending a year away, first in the dorm and then at Camp Dry Gulch, I wasn't ready to move back in under my mom's roof.

When I came back from camp and went to Rhema, I crashed with friends or slept on the couch in my dad's apartment. But when I re-enrolled in ORU, a better alternative came up. My sister Lorine lived right next to the campus. Well, not just my sister—there was also her husband, and her two kids. But while this was probably not what you would envision as an ideal situation for a college student, it was ideal for me. Okay, instead of a roommate, I shared a room with my sister's kids, and helped watch them whenever I could in return for room and board. It wasn't exactly conducive to a "wild and crazy college experience," but it enabled me to stay in school, and that was the most important thing for me. Keeping my eyes on the prize. Putting one foot in front of the other. Letting God take care of the rest.

The third issue, of course, was getting the money to pay my actual tuition. I needed to apply for financial aid again — and again, I made the rounds of all the possible places and organizations that might give money to a young man in my situation. By this point, I had basically become an expert at filling out forms. Which has actually turned out to be a pretty important skill to have.

The thing about agencies and forms is, they (the agencies) tend to lose them (the forms). And when they do, it's not like they call you up, apologize profusely and ask what they can do to make it better. If you want something that involves fixing the bureaucracy, it's up to you. So keep a file folder with copies of *everything*. I promise, you'll thank me for this advice later.

The final issue for me was finding another job, since, after putting in a few years under the Golden Arches, I was ready for a change. Luckily, when my youth pastor from church got a visit from the franchisee of the Chick-fil-A location at the Woodland Hills Mall looking for recruits, he thought of me. Then he called me and told me about Chick-fil-A.

And the rest…as they say…is history.

Chick-fil-A may be a quick-service restaurant, but any similarities to Mickey D's pretty much end there. First of all, Chick-fil-A, Inc. is a company with a business philosophy based on Biblical principles — which sets it apart from any other fast-food chain in the world that I know of. Honestly, what other quick-service restaurant do you know of that actually closes on Sundays? That's giving up a lot of revenue just because you believe it's the right thing to do…but at Chick-fil-A, it is part of the business model.

And it's not just about philosophy. It's also about food. At Chick-fil-A, most of the food is made fresh, in the restaurant. Each piece of chicken is hand-breaded, instead of coming to the restaurant in those frozen, pre-breaded patties some of the other quick-service restaurants use.

The work situation itself is also different. Instead of working for some random manager who may or may not really care about the business, at Chick-fil-A chain restaurants, you work directly for a franchised business owner — a person who cares about sales, profits and each individual team member.

I would learn just how much they care in the months to come.

CHAPTER 8
TIME TO MAKE
A CHANGE

If people like change so much, why do babies cry when it happens to them?

-Arthur Greeno

My employer wasn't the only thing that changed for me during my sophomore year at Oral Roberts. That was also the year I finally let go of my plans to become a youth pastor and embarked on what would be a totally different career path — toward commercial art.

Yes, I know. I realize this is a HUGE change for a guy who initially set out to work in a church for the rest of his life. But after struggling through all those classes that seemed to be all about arguing, to be completely honest, I decided I wanted to do something fun with my life. And I had just made the discovery that art was fun.

Actually, it was my experience working as a summer camp counselor that kind of sealed the deal. When I was at camp, I would draw these little cartoons, and discovered I really had a knack for being creative on paper (I know you're surprised). When I let myself dare to "go there" and think about what I really loved to do, I realized that what I loved more than anything were Disney films, and the way those animated characters came to life. And all those animators have to start somewhere, right?

So I decided to go for it. I would major in art and work for Disney. I went straight to my counselor and changed my major.

This in itself was not a big deal. The average college student actually changes their major three times during college. So one new major in two years—how drastic could that be? The real issue was that no one told me much about what being an art major would entail.

Most people don't just waltz into their counselor's office and walk out an art major without some preparation. Most art majors spend a lot of time in high school drawing and painting and developing their talent. Me, I took one pottery class in 9th grade—that was the pinnacle of my artistic education.

So, like most things I had embarked upon in my young life, my new major was going to be more of a challenge than I imagined.

I got a little more of a sense of what I had gotten myself into when I walked into my first art class—a three-dimensional design class. All I was required to bring with me was a pencil and paper, yet all of my classmates walked in with these massive portfolios filled with masterpieces representing years of study, along with colored pencils and other stuff real artists carry around with them.

It took me about 30 seconds to realize I was in way, way over my head. I think it took the professor even less time than that. But I had made a decision, I had followed my heart—there was no way I was turning back now.

I'll never forget my first assignment in that class. It sounded simple enough. We were supposed to take our initials, and do something "unique" with them on paper. "Unique" being the operative word.

I twiddled my pencil in my fingers and stared at the blank page for the longest time—waiting for inspiration to strike. I really, really wanted to prove that I belonged in that class, that it wasn't a mistake made by some kid who really should just become a youth pastor and forget about all this creativity stuff.

Finally, I came up with the idea to use a monkey and a palm tree to surround my initials (yes, a monkey. After the gorilla mask, you must think I have some sort of primate fixation). When I finished, I was actually quite proud of my work. The next day, I brought it to the front of the class to show the professor.

He was not impressed.

He called my work "cutesy" (it's amazing the things that your mind hangs on to sometimes). He said it was something you'd see on the back of a cereal box. Which, even though I was a commercial art major, and a cereal box was exactly the sort of place you'd see a piece of commercial art, was not the effect I was supposed to be going for. He wanted "unique," not "cutesy."

So I tried again. I took the assignment home with me and worked on it all night long. I brought my project in the next day…

…and got the exact same reaction. Whatever "unique" was, I definitely wasn't getting it. What did he want from me? What was I not getting?

When you try something twice and fail both times, you basically have two options. Well, three—you can give up, which for me was NOT an option. The other two are, you can keep doing the same thing you've been doing and hope to get a different result— something Einstein once said is the definition of insanity. Or you can try something completely different.

That's what I did. I just let go. I stopped holding back, stopped trying to figure out what "unique" meant and what the professor wanted and what on earth I was supposed to do—which clearly wasn't working—and drew whatever popped into my head. It was kind of like going crazy…except on paper. But then again, I'd never had a problem with crazy. Crazy…I was good at.

When the assignment was finally finished, even I couldn't see my initials anymore. I knew they were in there somewhere, but I had to look very closely to find them. Anyone would have to agree that I had certainly come up with something different—something…dare I say it…unique. It was definitely way too bizarre to ever make it to the back of a cereal box—even one of those all-natural, hippie cereals.

But would the professor actually like it? That was the million-dollar question.

When I brought the finished product into class, I was ready for the worst—ready for the professor to announce to the entire class that I really had no business in commercial art and toss me out of the room, admonishing me to never, ever, ever pick up a pencil again and to return to my youth pastor training program immediately.

But he didn't. He liked it.

I learned something important that day. Art class wasn't about delivering perfect, cereal-box-ready finished products. It was about exploring, about pushing the envelope as far as it could go, about opening my mind and just letting my creativity run wild.

In other words, it actually was a perfect fit for me. I was essentially given a green light to think the way that I normally thought, to see the world through my own, slightly-twisted eyes, and put it all down on paper (or in sculpture, or in paint) for other people to see. It was like sharing a peek into my world.

And so, that became my path. I threw myself into each project, pushing the envelope as far as it would go. I did some crazy projects (I know you're surprised). Once I made a pot about 2 feet big. It was very… symmetrical, and needed some creativity, so I beat it with a stick and got some cool designs on it. It looked great. I made a functioning teapot that was a guy upside down in a toilet in my ceramics class. We even lathered me up head to toe with Vaseline, and made a plaster mold of my body and painted it flourecent colors (I lost all my chest hair in that venture). And while I didn't turn out to be a great artist—you won't find any of my work hanging in a museum between the Picassos and the Monets—my time as an art major taught me another important life lesson. It taught me to trust my instincts. It taught me to resist the urge to put a lid on my imagination, and instead let it run wild. Those lessons proved to be very valuable to me later in life.

(To be very honest, one piece I helped with was displayed at the Philbrook Museum of Art for a short time, until it sold. It was a Christmas tree made of glass ornaments we made at the Glassblowing studio.)

But before any of that happened, I had to get through another major challenge. But this one, no amount of training or hard work or really anything could prepare me for.

It happened during my junior year in college. I was staying with Mike, working three or four jobs to make ends meet and get through school. And I got one of those phone calls you can't possibly imagine—the kind that means your life will never be the same.

My little sister Kathleen had been hit by a car—and she wasn't expected to pull through.

This was especially tragic because Kathleen had just managed to turn her life around. After having two children by two different fathers before she was 18, she had gotten serious about school, earned her high school diploma and decided she was going to become a nurse.

She was on her way to Dallas to check out a nursing school when the car she was riding in was involved in a minor accident. The accident itself was no big deal. But while she stood on the side of the road waiting for the police to come, another car drove by, swerved at the sight of the scene, lost control, and struck her.

She was barely 18 years old.

I don't remember much about the phone call. I was told Kathleen had been rushed to the hospital in Dallas with severe injuries. I took off right away—I grabbed Lorine and borrowed a car, there was no way mine would make the drive—and headed to Dallas as fast as I could go. But even if the car had suddenly sprouted wings, it wouldn't have been enough. My little sister died before I made it to Dallas to say goodbye. I never got a chance to tell her I loved her one more time.

It didn't seem fair. Still, as horrible I as felt, however much pain I was in, I needed to accept what had happened.

It wasn't easy for any of us. My mother was in hysterics. My father was shattered. Now that I'm a father, I can only imagine how horrible it would be to outlive your own child. My older sister, who was also a parent, was helping me hold it together.

But there was one more, very real problem—in addition to grief and shock—facing the four of us. There was the issue of my sister's body. We couldn't just leave her there, in a strange city, hundreds of miles away. But the cheapest option to give her any sort of dignity in death was cremation. And that would cost between $500 and $600.

If you remember anything I've told you about my parents, you can probably guess they didn't have that kind of money lying around. Or even in a bank, saved for an emergency.

The same went for my sister, who was tapped out caring for her two kids. Which left me, a struggling college student who was working three or four jobs, depending on which month it was, and barely scraping by, to take care of it.

So I did something I'd never done before.

I asked Mike to help me.

I called him and poured out my story of everything that had happened. He instantly expressed his sympathies, and then I explained the financial issue. We discussed the fact that I needed that money and that I had nothing right then. He told me he'd get back to me in half an hour.

But as it turns out, I didn't need that half an hour. While I waited for Mike, that old problem-solving instinct—the one that got me to summer camp after my sophomore year in high school, the one that kept me at ORU against the odds—kicked in.

Like many college students who paid their own bills, I was actually in possession of my very own credit card. I think my credit limit was probably around $400, and I'm positive whatever that credit limit was, I was maxed out. But I had the card. And if I had the card, I had a potential solution.

I turned the card over and called the customer service number on the back. It didn't take long for me to find myself on the line with an actual human being—this was the late '80s after all, so companies still had real, live customer service agents answering phones and talking to people.

I explained my situation to the person on the other end and asked if there was any way that they could raise the limit on my card. I told them what I would need.

To my surprise, they agreed.

I learned a very valuable lesson that day. If you really need something, there's never any harm in asking for it.

I never thought that a company would do something like that, especially for a college student who was struggling just to make ends meet. So here's a shout-out to Citibank, because they did it for me.

Not long after I hung up, Mike called. He, Mark and Darrell had come up with the money for me. I don't know from where, but they had. I explained to him that I didn't need it, and I didn't—but what he'd given me meant so much more. My friends showed me what it really means to have true friends—people who will stand by you through thick and thin. After everything I had been through, after all my struggles, I really was not alone. I was surrounded by people who loved me and who had my back. It meant everything to me.

So ultimately, while I may not have been able to say goodbye to my sister, I was able to help ease her passage from this world. We had Kathleen cremated, and we brought her ashes home to Tulsa. In that way, by bringing Kathleen home, I was able to tell her how much I loved her one last time. Kathleen had a son, Chris, who was 3 at the time and went to live with his father, and a daughter, Tab who went to live with her father after briefly staying with my mother.

After all that drama, it did take some time for me to get back to normal. I had been through a major shock and a family tragedy, but I really had no option other than to keep going, showing up for class, doing my homework, working those three or four jobs so I could pay my bills.

The good news was that one of those jobs was at a Chick-fil-A restaurant.

My boss at Chick-fil-A, Ben Clark, the franchise operator of the Woodland Hills Mall restaurant where I worked, had seen what I'd been through and knew how hard I'd been struggling. Between school, Kathleen's death and working like a maniac, my life must not have looked like much fun to an outsider. So when my boss saw an opportunity for me to get out of Tulsa and away from my troubles for a while, he told me about it.

A new Chick-fil-A restaurant was set to open in St. Louis. No doubt you're probably thinking, "So what, Arthur? Companies open new locations all the time — that's called business, right?" But in the Chick-fil-A system, a grand opening is a grand celebration, like the birth of a new baby, or Thanksgiving or the Fourth of July.

How big a celebration? There are games and prizes and all kinds of excitement. And in the midst of all of it, they would have me — dressed in a chicken suit (this was way before the Chick-fil-A Cows). For a kid who loved nothing more than going out in public in a gorilla mask, spending a few days dressed as Doodles the Chicken, and meeting new people in a new city, was way better than therapy (except for the part of the Doodles outfit that required me to wear panty hose — I can't say I really enjoyed that).

Staying in a nice hotel and getting taken out to eat in nice restaurants each night was the icing on the cake. But the best part, the very best part of the trip, was the things I learned about Chick-fil-A, Inc. and its franchise system.

My trip to St. Louis exposed me not just to franchise operators like my boss and the operator of the new St. Louis restaurant, but to Chick-fil-A, Inc's corporate staff. Spending time with them, I got my first glimpse into the corporate culture of Chick-fil-A. I saw firsthand, both from my boss at the Woodland Hills Mall location and from the corporate office team, how Chick-fil-A operators banded together and how everyone looked out for each other. I also learned more about a whole other world within the Chick-fil-A system — about the leaders of the company who plan and develop all of the restaurants, who work with marketing and customer relations, and who basically help the chain expand and grow.

And a little light bulb went off in my head.

Maybe, when I grew up, I could be one of them.

CHAPTER 9
SENIOR YEAR

People often say that motivation doesn't last. Well, neither does bathing — that's why we recommend it daily
— Zig Ziglar

I don't know how it happened (well, yes I do — studying, working hard, applying myself) but suddenly there I was, just a single semester away from graduating from Oral Roberts University and starting my real, adult life. I had beaten the odds, I had left my difficult childhood behind and forged my own destiny — with God's help, of course. Now it was time to get ready for the next step.

By this time, the whole plan to work for Disney — the reason I had switched my major to commercial art in the first place — wasn't looking quite as tempting. A girl from ORU had done exactly what I had planned to do. She graduated with an art degree and parlayed it into a job with the entertainment giant. At this point, her job consisted of bringing coffee to executives — and she'd been doing this for two years! I know starting at the bottom is a great American tradition, but there was no way I was going to be a coffee girl.

I should probably clarify that. I hear many people say things like, "That job is beneath me," or "I went to school for a degree, I'm not serving coffee." I promise you, none of that was an issue to me. There were just two reasons I knew I couldn't take that kind of job.

First of all, I don't like coffee, and second, I'm not a girl.

The summer of my Junior year, I went to Little Rock Arkansas, where at night I was a manager for one of the Chick-fil-A locations, and during the day I did an internship for a company doing Computer Animation. There were no computer animation places in Tulsa, and in 1990 computers were a little scarcer than they are today. This was cutting edge. So I had set myself up to move forward on that path… but something kept drawing me away from art.

At the same time, I had continued to rise through the ranks at the Chick-fil-A restaurant in Tulsa where I worked. It had been easy for me — coming in as a team member from that "other" fast food place, I had the technical skills down already, and all too well. I knew about filling drinks, sweeping floors, wiping tables and stuff, so it was fairly natural growing into the role of team leader at Chick-fil-A and training new employees the same way I had been trained.

My job was just another place to do what I always tried to strive for with the rest of my life. It was all about doing what needed to be done, being trustworthy and dependable, looking for areas to be an asset, and always trying to do my best. And it paid off. I became a night manager, and later, when my college schedule changed, I was made a day manager. And the more I learned about this franchise system for the Owner-Operator, and the more time I spent there, the more I felt at home.

Actually, my connection to Chick-fil-A was really cemented the year before, with that trip to St. Louis. That was when I experienced the Chick-fil-A, Inc. Corporate Office on a deeper level, and learned about all the jobs I hadn't known existed before that not only provided support to the franchisees, but also kept the entire Chick-fil-A system going and growing. Those jobs included marketing — so it seemed like a natural next step. Instead of marketing for Disney, I would do marketing for Chick-fil-A, Inc. But as my graduation date drew nearer, no corporate office marketing job materialized (the program I had been interested in disappeared), leaving me wondering what to do next.

My last semester at ORU was kind of a weird one anyway — since I sat out my first semester of my sophomore year, my friends had all graduated and I had one semester left to go. Mark, Darrell and Mike got an apartment together, and while I moved in with them,

I was still living the same life that they had just left behind — going to school and working at my college jobs. It would keep going like that until December.

That semester, when I was kind of on my own, I really started looking at other ways to make a career within the Chick-fil-A system.

And I set my sights on another goal. I would join the corporate office in the role of a Business Intern. I am sure the legal department has a real technical way to describe this position, but for those of us on the streets, we knew that this was the position for people to go out and run company-operated restaurants that, how shall we say...needed some love.

Never mind the fact that I was still a college senior, or that I had no money to buy in to a Chick-fil-A franchise. The Woodland Hills Mall store at the time had multiple Business Interns in it, and it was *my* store (sounds like a typical entitled college kid doesn't it?). I had seen Owner-Operators come and go from this location, but I was still there. I could run the place with one eye closed and one hand tied behind my back — at least in my own mind. I felt...and this is a dirty word but I'm going to say it here anyway...*entitled*.

I forgot that I didn't get there alone. It's not that I lost my faith — ever. God and Jesus Christ remained the focus of my life, and they do to this day. I still went to church. I still prayed every day. I studied the Bible, listened to Christian music and surrounded myself with Godly people.

Luckily, the good people at Chick-fil-A were about to remind me of one unforgettable fact. I was not in charge.

For starters, even though I felt I had worked at the Woodland location the longest, even though I had seen franchised-operators, Temporary Managers and Business Interns come and go, even though I was still there and felt entitled, like I deserved it - the powers-that-be at Chick-fil-A would not simply hand over the keys to Woodland Hills. If I wanted to run a company-operated restaurant, I would have to apply for it, just like everyone else, as a Business Intern. In the long run, my goal was to be a franchised-operator, but I was coached that this was the only way I had a chance, so I went down this path.

Having navigated the massive bureaucracy of the college financial aid system for more than four years, I had yet to meet a form I couldn't fill out convincingly. And what could possibly be on a Chick-fil-A application anyway? I'd applied for jobs before. It's usually not a big deal. You fill in your name, birth date, education, previous work experience and stuff like that. Maybe you give a couple of references who will vouch for what a great guy (or gal) you are. Maybe you have a résumé you attach with it. Maybe you even do it online, from the comfort of your own home, in your pajamas (of course in those days, computers were kinda hard to find).

That's not quite how they do it at Chick-fil-A.

At least, it wasn't way back in the early '90s.

Applying for a Chick-fil-A, Inc. corporate position was probably a lot like applying to be an agent in the CIA. They wanted a LOT of information. Just the sheer amount of work required was exhausting. It was sort of like taking an entire college class in one sitting. The paperwork made the most complex college essays look like a third grade report on "What I Did on My Summer Vacation." There were piles and piles and piles of paperwork—probably an entire forest was sacrificed to make a single Chick-fil-A corporate application. In fact, the Chick-fil-A franchise application required just as much work, and to this day, whenever I come across someone who has applied for a Chick-fil-A franchise, the one comment they make is about how huge the Operator Packet is!

What did they want to know about me on all those papers? In a word—everything. They wanted to know where I grew up. Where I went to school. What I did with my spare time. If I'd ever tried to steal a Luke Skywalker toy.

Okay, they didn't exactly ask that one. But, having grown up the way I grew up, this kind of intensive probing into my background was still a little scary. What if, given my colorful past, I didn't make the grade?

However, one thing I learned from my dad was that no one wanted to hear my "garbage" (okay…his words were a little more colorful). Unless it was brought up, I did not discuss it. So my "secrets" remained safe with me.

Then, there was the issue of the photo. Chick-fil-A asked for one, right on the application.

Still, this may sound like nothing to you—since you can probably snap a photo of this book, right now, with your phone.

But back in the early 1990s (I'm really starting to sound like an old man here, aren't I?), there was no such thing as a phone that took your picture, or computers that printed your photos, or webcams. We didn't even have DVDs and still listened to music on cassette tapes, not that that has anything to do with this story…

At that point during my senior year, I was not in possession of any photograph of myself that would convince Chick-fil-A that I was capable of running a store. I wasn't about to send a shot of me in a gorilla mask! And I didn't have a portfolio filled with attractive headshots sitting around (Arthur smiling, Arthur looking thoughtful, Arthur in a tie, Arthur in a sweater…) to use for such an occasion. I briefly thought I would send my senior picture from high school, but that seemed, well…not very businesslike. Bottom line—I would need to come up with a decent picture of myself. So I did what anyone in my circumstance would do—I asked my buddy Mike for help.

Coming from a more "upscale" background, Mike had one thing that I didn't have that I needed for my photo—decent clothes. So I borrowed his nice suit, a shirt and even a red power tie to complete the look. Then I went to slip into his pants…and realized that there was no way they were going to fit.

The result? I sent the top brass at Chick-fil-A a photo of me in a shirt, jacket, tie…and boxer shorts. Not that anyone could tell. I had Mike frame the shot from the waist up.

If you happen to be from the Corporate Office, don't bother looking it up. Well, you can if you want, but even though you now know the secret, you still won't be able to see my Super Grover boxers in the picture.

Once the photo was taken, I finished the application by specifying the store I wanted—the Woodland Hills Mall store where I had been working. You know, the one I thought I was entitled to! Of course, I was not stupid—I put other locations down as alternates in case, for some reason, I could not have my first choice store. While writing this book, the legal department looked it up, and they said I requested the "Tulsa" area.

Then the real fun started.

It was time for the interviews.

I'd been through interviews before. I'd sit down with a manager of some sort and talk about the job and my work experience. Maybe I'd be in the room for ten minutes. They weren't particularly stressful... or involved. Most of the time, I didn't even break a sweat.

With Chick-fil-A, Inc. it was different. First off, they actually flew me to Atlanta, where the Chick-fil-A headquarters is located. Second, they put me up in a hotel...because third (and this is the only NOT fun part), I would be sitting for a series of interviews over a couple of very long days.

The process was stressful...and exhausting. The interviews were intense, with the interviewers asking me question after question, forcing me to think on my feet. It was almost like they were waiting for me to slip up and prove that I didn't deserve an internship, that I couldn't handle it, that allowing me to continue on this path would be a huge mistake.

And honestly, why wouldn't it be? I was barely 22 years old. I had no savings or investments where I could come up with the money to invest in my own store at that point—and no rich uncle to invest in me and get me started. And beyond that, I had no formal business training—I was a commercial art major! Basically, I was just a kid with a few years of fast food experience who came up with the crazy idea of eventually buying his own franchise.

A couple of the interviews really made me nervous. I remember one in particular—they were doing construction on the building, so there was literally pounding on the wall, hammering, sawing and all kinds of noise going on in the background. It was hard to hear, so the person interviewing me kept having me repeat things, and in my already nervous brain, I started questioning if I was the right man for the job. Was he asking me to repeat it because he could not hear it, or because I said something not appropriate (which with my background was very possible)?

In another interview, the guy asking the questions actually nodded off (just for a second, but it did happen)! I just sat there wondering how I should handle it…until he woke up with a start and finished the interview (FYI—never schedule an interview after lunch).

In other words, the process was just a *little* nerve-wracking…

Still, I absolutely felt I deserved the Woodland Hills mall store, that I had somehow earned the right to run that business on my own at the age of 22, that all I had to do was get through the interviews, and within a few weeks the Chick-fil-A bosses would show up at my door with a big bouquet of balloons and a band…and a key.

But that's not exactly what happened.

I got a phone call, which, honestly, was the most likely scenario anyway. So, that part was not a surprise. While Chick-fil-A did have a store for me, it was not the Woodland Hills Mall restaurant that I had put so much of myself into. It was the Eastland Mall location. Woodland Hills had been franchised to someone else to be the Operator, and he would go through training after I did. Eastland Mall—that restaurant was ranked fourth *to last* out of all of the Chick-fil-A stores *in the world*. Yes, it was that bad.

So what did I do? I took the offer. I was hurt, and my ego was a bit bruised, but I understood. (Nowadays, Chick-fil-A gets over 20,000 Operator inquiries a year, to fill less than 100 restaurant openings. So yes, I was lucky even to be a Business Intern). I also knew this could be a stepping stone to greater things. Some of my friends and family thought taking this store was beneath me, but I really felt like I could make this happen. I always loved the long shot!

Within a few weeks, I was back in Atlanta at Chick-fil-A headquarters for training. It was there, finally, that I realized just how arrogant, delusional and just plain crazy I had been. I was the only

22-year-old college senior in the group. These were real-live business people, with experience and fancy degrees and money and families and mortgages. They weren't people who shared an apartment with their three college buddies. And I seriously doubt any of them posed for pictures in their underwear.

As you might imagine, I learned a lot at that training session. I learned all the standard stuff, like about the history of their company and their philosophy, along with their strategies for running a business and dealing with customers and employees.

But I also learned something a lot more important. I learned that there is no such thing as "entitled." Seeing all those other people, and realizing just how much I had to learn and how very small I was, my humility finally returned. God had allowed me to get this far *despite* my attitude. Then, as always, He was in charge, not me.

After training, management decided that I would still be getting the Eastland Mall's Chick-fil-A restaurant. Deep down inside, I was still hoping to prove myself and get Woodland, but that was yet to come.

Of course, I did have some warning. On my way out, one of the training instructors (I will not mention names to protect the innocent) actually sat me down in his office and told me point blank that management "had some concerns about me."

Ouch.

Not surprising — to be honest, I also had some concerns about me! But still...ouch.

I heard a quote once, "never miss a good opportunity to shut up," but I didn't learn that until later in life, and unfortunately during the training I missed a lot of those opportunities.

The truth hurts. Suddenly, images of my grandfather telling me I would never amount to anything flashed in my head, along with a few of my many other failures. But I swallowed hard and focused on the task at hand.

The thing was, I really wasn't confident in taking on the responsibility. No matter how many rabbits I had pulled out of my hat so far, running a business is…well…serious business. And I couldn't afford to be an Operator at the time anyway. In order to do that, I would actually have to buy into a franchise. The initial fee was $5,000, which isn't really an enormous amount of money, considering that I would then be able to own and operate my own franchised restaurant business. But at that point, it might as well have been five million dollars, because I didn't have it. As a matter of fact, I didn't even have a car! I had given my old heap to my sister, who needed it even more than I did.

As it turned out, being a Business Intern would be the best of both worlds for me. It protected Chick-fil-A while giving me an opportunity to learn the ropes. It was almost like an extension of college—I was training for my future career, but getting paid for it at the same time. I knew in my heart that as long as I worked hard and did my very best, I would, someday, be a Chick-fil-A franchise Operator.

As long as I remembered to let Him lead the way. A constant struggle God and I have to this day.

My adult life had finally started.

Set your goals
so you know which
direction you're going.

Making small steps
toward your goal is not
exciting, but it's still moving
you closer to your goal.

Over time you can look back
at those small steps and realize
how far you came.

CHAPTER 10
HOW TO SUCCEED IN BUSINESS BY REALLY, REALLY, *REALLY* TRYING

It's easier to succeed than fail.
— *S. Truett Cathy*

If God was planning to teach me a lesson about feeling entitled, the Chick-fil-A at Eastland Mall was a great place to start the learning process. It offered what I now like to call an "opportunity-rich environment."

You know how some neighborhoods have a "good" mall, with a great layout and great stores where people like to hang out, and a "bad" mall, where people only go when they need something specific from a specific store or want to see a movie that's only playing there? Eastland was that "bad" mall.

First off, the developer had designed it to look like a circus tent — definitely not an upscale destination mall where people actually liked to hang out. It wasn't just goofy-looking, it was also uncomfortable. The roof leaked when it rained, it was cold inside when it snowed outside, and when the sun set, the entire mall looked dark and dreary.

But for my purposes, the very worst part of this very bad mall was *my* part of the mall — the food court. It was hidden, along with the movie theater, down below the main level where all the stores were. We actually called it the "dungeon," just to give you an idea of how warm and inviting it was. That location basically meant that unless people were hungry and specifically looking for something to eat, they wouldn't even pass by Chick-fil-A. They wouldn't even know I was there.

The silver lining to this cloud was that left a lot of room for improvement.

If it puts it into perspective, I do more sales in a month currently than Eastland did in a year.

I just needed to figure out how to get more people down to the dungeon to try what I had to offer. I figured that once people actually tasted the amazing, delicious food that Chick-fil-A had to offer (a shameless plug, but still true!), it would pretty much sell itself.

This meant I needed to try what we in the quick-service food biz call "sampling." If you've ever been to a mall and had someone from one of the food stores offer you a little piece of food—say, for example, a piece of chicken on a toothpick—that's "sampling." The restaurant gives you free food, introducing you to our "hero" product, the Chick-fil-A Chicken Sandwich, hoping you'll like it so much you'll buy your lunch, or dinner, or midday snack there, instead of at one of the other food court stores. And it works! It's actually the most effective way to market your food, especially in a food court. The other dungeon dwellers did not like how impactful it was in my business, but instead of doing it themselves they chose to just sit there and complain.

One challenge was getting the samples to the customers. Most quick-service restaurants offer samples right in front of their location in the mall, but at Eastland, this was a very non-productive option. Chick-fil-A was downstairs, in the dungeon, while all the customers were upstairs, where the stores were. You had to go down a 60-foot escalator to get there. The only way to make sure my samples actually *got* sampled was to bring them upstairs, where the customers were, hoping they'd like it enough to come down to the dungeon for more.

I had the brilliant (not!) idea of using a little cart, filling it up with samples and rolling it to stores upstairs and sample off their lease line. Since we had virtually no budget, I thought building my own rolling cart out of wood was cheaper than buying a nice stainless steel one for $250. It was a great plan, and should have worked in theory (my managers and wife always wince when I say "theoretically"). So we set out on my initial voyage, cart filled with everything needed, including hot samples of our delicious Chick-fil-A Chicken Sandwich, and then it happened: my homemade cart hit a crack in the tile floor and the whole thing buckled—hard. I ended up laying on my belly on the table that was flat on the floor, chicken parts, nails, pieces of wood, and my ego everywhere. I just rolled over and laughed.

What can I say? I was never much of a carpenter.

By the end of the year, due to sampling and other crazy antics, we were up 38% from the year before.

Meanwhile, my romantic life was blossoming—becoming a little more serious. I had been dating a girl who was not good for me, while Noell, that cute girl I met in my youth group about nine years before, had become my best friend. We told each other everything—including everything about my horrible girlfriend and her equally horrible boyfriend. Eventually, we decided to dump our respective significant others—and when the deeds were done, in true "When Harry Met Sally" fashion, we called each other immediately with all the details.

It was all completely innocent. We considered each other friends. Best friends. We weren't planning to go out or anything. But there was this weird, nagging feeling. We got along so well. We liked being together so much. So eventually, we wound up on an official "date."

You know those dates where fireworks go off and romantic music plays and you realize that you've found the love of your life? My first date with Noell didn't feel like that. It felt weird. Especially the part where we kissed—it was kind of like kissing my sister.

So we decided not to do that again for a while.

After a couple of weeks we got over it. And we've been together ever since.

Meanwhile, I got a piece of not-exactly-pleasant news. I learned that Chick-fil-A was now looking for a franchisee...for the Eastland Mall restaurant. I was not a happy camper. In fact, I was basically an *enraged* camper.

Eastland was *my* store. I was the one who had gone down into the dungeon and taken over and brought my samples upstairs and turned the store around. I was the one who boosted sales by 38%, remember? Me, Arthur Greeno! And now they were preparing to give *my* store to someone else???

No way. Not on my watch.

I picked up the phone and called company headquarters in Atlanta. I told them I wasn't happy with their decision to offer the store to someone other than me. I'd like to say I did it in the nicest way possible, but I can't be certain that's true. I was pretty upset. But the powers-that-be back in Atlanta had a pretty good reason for not offering the store to me. They reminded me that, back when I had applied to be a Business Intern, not a franchisee, I wasn't interested in Eastland. I only had eyes for Woodland Hills Mall.

That may have been true back then, but I really, really, *really* wanted it now. I had made it mine. How could I let them give it away?

I was able to convince the home office, and I was, at last, offered the Eastland Mall store. I had proven myself. I could be trusted as a Chick-fil-A Operator.

There was just one small problem left to deal with. The required initial investment is $5,000 to buy into Chick-fil-A as a franchised Operator. That's not a whole lot considering the benefits, but it was about $4,999 more than I had. If I was going to realize my dream and accomplish what I'd been trying to accomplish since my senior year at ORU, I needed to raise some money.

I wasn't really worried about how I would do this. After everything I'd already overcome, I had learned one thing. There is always a way. God made sure of that. I just had to figure out what that way was.

For me, that meant taking out a loan at 19% interest (I really had no credit to speak of other than one credit card). Was it the smartest financial decision I ever made? Maybe not. But at the age of 22, I became the franchised Operator of the Eastland Mall Chick-fil-A restaurant. I was a bona-fide business owner.

Now, I had to deal with the responsibilities that came with being a bona-fide business owner.

Running the Eastland Mall Chick-fil-A restaurant as an intern was different than running the same restaurant as a franchised Operator. Suddenly, I was personally responsible for payroll taxes, for insurance and all the other "operating costs" associated with owning a business that the home office used to handle for me. All of that had to be taken care of *before* I would even see a profit. And since Eastland was a small, low-revenue store, controlling costs to the point where I could make any profit at all was a major issue.

What was going wrong? I thought my years of working at Chick-fil-A restaurants, both as an employee of an Operator, and during my employment with Chick-fil-A, Inc. as a Business Intern, had taught me everything I needed to know about running my own Chick-fil-A. Instead I was struggling to wrap my brain around this business. As I dealt with situations involving the corporate office I often felt I was not taken seriously (this may or may not have been true, but as a somewhat insecure young leader this is how I felt).

Frustrated, I finally turned to one of the men I really respected and humbly asked him his opinion. I felt I would either get what I was looking for, or show weakness, and open myself up for problems later. I took the gamble and it paid off—his advice was pretty surprising. He said the problem wasn't that I was young, or that I didn't have a business degree.

The problem, according to this guy, was the way I dressed! Seriously?

It wasn't like I showed up for work in jeans and an old t-shirt. I wore a nice shirt, tie and pants, like Chick-fil-A had encouraged us to. I tried to look professional. I certainly didn't look like a slob...

I did not understand, and so I questioned him. He, in a very professional manner politely told me that I needed to read the book *Dressing for Success*, and I would understand. He was right. And once I'd finished it and absorbed all the tips it had to offer, I went out and spent two thousand dollars on a new wardrobe. I got a great suit, and many other outfits to go with it.

Yes, it was a lot of money. But it was definitely worth it. Previously, I would buy my shirts and pants at Wal Mart, which is fine for general use, but in a professional environment, they just would not stand up.

When I put on that suit, it was kind of like when Superman put on his cape. Suddenly, I wasn't Arthur Greeno, struggling 22-year-old recent college grad. I was Arthur Greeno, Businessman! I felt powerful. I felt strong. And the confidence I felt inside started to show on the outside.

My talk with my "advisor" also taught me the value of not fearing to ask questions. He didn't actually tell me this, but based on our last activity, I figured it out. You've probably heard the word "networking" being tossed around, but you might not know exactly what it means. Basically, it's just the business term for talking with other people for business purposes—they can be colleagues, they can be competitors, they can even be people who have nothing to do with *your* business, but are simply *in* business. The idea is that when you talk with people about your businesses, you share stories and ideas, creating a "network" of people who support each other. And everyone involved is better for it. So I started learning from the other operators' successes.

I learned there are a lot of great business books out there, and started inhaling them. In the past I would read about one book every two years; now, after seeing direct results from books, I started slow: (for me) three per year, five per year. Now I believe I will pick up at least 9-10 per year (mostly audio, but still the content is the same).

I put a lot of work into marketing my business, trying free sandwich giveaways, marketing stunts, anything I could to draw more customers down to the Eastland dungeon. And once they got there, I made it my goal to run the cleanest, quickest, friendliest, best food store in the mall — so that people would come back, and tell their friends, and my business would continue to grow.

Speaking of growing, my relationship with Noell was getting stronger and stronger until, at the tender age of 23, I knew I could hold her off no longer. I could tell she wanted me to ask her to marry me every time I saw her; I was so hot and studly, I couldn't blame her (again, I believe this is called the author's prerogative, and if you ask Noell about this and get a different answer, well then you'll know the truth!).

How do you ask the most important person in your life the most important question you'll ever ask in your life? I wanted to do it right. For a person known for wild, creative gestures, that required a plan.

Noell and I worked at a youth group together, and a new youth center was scheduled for a Grand Opening. That meant a stage, a crowd, and people. It was perfect. The day of the opening, I swung by Noell's house and asked her parents for permission to marry their daughter. Lucky for me, they gave the okay. Then, that night at the opening, in front of a crowd of about 300 people, I proposed to the woman I love.

I fully expected her to burst into tears, throw her arms around me and scream "yes" at the top of her lungs.

Instead, she just looked at me and said, "What?"

NOT the reaction I was going for.

The problem was, the kids were screaming so loudly, she couldn't hear my proposal. She really had no idea what I said. Luckily, when she figured it out, she did say yes. Otherwise, the whole thing would have been pretty embarrassing.

Now, things were about to get *really* crazy.

I had made such a success of the Eastland Mall Chick-fil-A restaurant that some of the other Operators had actually started coming to me for advice — and some of them even had business degrees! The corporate office in Atlanta also noticed. I decided it was time for me to move up to a bigger restaurant at the Tulsa Promenade Mall. The Operator of that store had just moved on, and so I asked for it, and was granted the right to establish a new business at that restaurant location.

Planning a wedding and taking over a new business at the same time was a huge undertaking—especially since the Promenade store was kind of a mess. Luckily, most wedding planning falls to the bride—if the groom is smart, she does most of it and he just sits back and asks, "How much?" and, "Where should I stand?" So Noell did pretty much everything, and in between meetings with florists and caterers, she was right by my side, scrubbing down walls at the Tulsa Promenade Mall.

Not exactly the most romantic way to plan for a wedding…but it made that day when we finally exchanged vows at Grace Church—the church I had attended since I was a junior in high school—that much sweeter. At the age of 24, I was a married man.

We moved into a duplex on the rough side of town. How rough? Well, a man was murdered two doors down. The cross-dressing prostitute kept walking his (or her) poodle across our yard. The bag lady lived next door, and my dog bit her when she was walking her cart in front of my house one night. One-eyed George lived across one street, the housing projects were across the other street, and some doped-up weirdo kept hanging out on our porch because the voices told him to.

At least it was cheap!

Meanwhile, I was busy transforming the Chick-fil-A at Tulsa Promenade into *my* store. I had read in the newspaper that a major, 20-screen movie complex was going to be built across the street, as well as a new strip center with some big-box stores. I knew this meant traffic in the mall—and business for us—was going to jump. But I still wanted to make money in the meantime! So I did whatever I could to attract customers to my store. I ran games and gave away prizes, I set up displays with little mechanical chickens running around in circles on a table, sampled like a fiend—anything that might make someone stop just long enough to notice the tantalizing aroma wafting from the nearby Chick-fil-A restaurant.

By 1996, I was generating enough income from the operation of my business for us to move away from the Scary Neighborhood to a gingerbread house in midtown. It wasn't huge—just 1600 square feet—but perfect for us. And by "us," I mean me, Noell and baby Connor, who also came along in 1996.

Around this time, I decided to pursue my next challenge—the Chick-fil-A Symbol of Success Award. In order to win, I had to do what I did best, which was boost sales. That year I was able to do a 17% increase in sales, which helped me win that award.

I was thrilled to win the first year and drive the Ford of my choice, a new Mustang, around town. It was an awesome car. But the second year, when it came time to meet the challenge again and make the arrangement permanent by meeting my Symbol Sales goal and hanging onto the car for life, something even more important came up.

Who is mentoring you?
Reading my story, you can see
how many mentors I had
throughout my life.
Do you like to learn and
laugh at the same time?

Are you an entrepreneur
or just stuck and looking
for some people to sow
wisdom in your life?

Join myself and some friends of
mine that hold the same passion.
At **www.thrive15.com** you will
meet success stories like myself,
David Robinson (*yes, the basketball
legend*), Clay Clark and Pulitzer Prize
winner Clifton Taulbert, along with
many others who have a passion to teach
what we have learned to help others
overcome obstacles.

If you would like to join us,
use this code for a 1 month Free Trial!

www.thrive15.com
code: 2inspire

CHAPTER 11
WHAT I HAVE LEARNED

Success is…knowing your purpose in life, growing to reach your maximum potential, and sowing seeds that benefit others.
— *John C Maxwell*

What could be more important than winning a free car? If you're ever lucky enough to be able to ask yourself this question… well…congratulations in advance. And good luck. Making choices can be challenging—especially if it's a choice between one good thing and another good thing.

Reaching a point where I, Arthur Greeno, had that kind of choice to make was basically a miracle. With my background, with my upbringing, with my brief but terrifying childhood flirtation with a life of crime, I could have ended up anywhere. But by putting my life in the Lord's hands (and, of course, working my butt off) here I was, still in my 20's, choosing between two amazing rewards.

On one hand, I was eligible to win the Symbol of Success award for a second year and keep my beloved Mustang forever. But on the other hand, the Chick-fil-A restaurant where my odyssey had begun—the Woodland Hills Mall store that I had so wanted to make my own—was finally available to me. And I could only win the Symbol of Success award again if I stayed at the Promenade Mall location.

I like to think the fact that Woodland Hills was a higher volume store with a huge amount of potential for growth influenced my decision. But maybe it was the fact that Noell was pregnant again with our second child…and the thought of adding yet another car seat to the back of the Mustang sounded like more trouble than it was worth! As it was, I had to flip Connor's car seat upside down in order to make it fit (obviously empty, otherwise Connor would have gotten sick every time I put him in the car!).

So I gave up the car and my Tulsa Promenade business and finally, finally became the franchise Operator of the Chick-fil-A of the Woodland Hills Mall.

That was in July. In August, Noell gave birth to baby Casey. Would I ever have an opportunity to grow my business at a time when there wasn't some major event taking place in my personal life? I guess God knows I can handle it!

It was, however, a lot to handle. The store at Woodland Hills was another mess — which is sometimes the case when you're brought in to take over a store. A lot of the time, it happens because something went wrong, other times it's just because a new person has come in with a new set of eyes, and has different priorities.

In this case, the problems were mostly about morale. The interim manager who was running the store between the time when the previous Operator left and when I got there was not happy that her career with Chick-fil-A was ending, and she took it out on me, scaring all the employees by telling them that when I took over, I was planning on firing all of them and starting fresh.

The craziest thing about this story is the way I found out this was going on. One night just before I was set to take over, I got a phone call from a woman who I had never met, asking me if I planned to fire her! I told her that since I'd never met her, I certainly didn't have any reason to fire her — or anyone else, for that matter.

She wound up becoming one my very best mall managers.

Too bad she was the only employee I had a chance to talk to. On my first day, most of my employees didn't even bother showing up, they were so sure I was going to fire them anyway. So, I was there essentially all by myself with a million things to fix.

With employees constantly calling in sick, or not showing up, I was the one picking up the slack. I was really struggling. I reached a point where I actually asked the corporate office to help me out with wages. They told me they were not able to. I almost handed in my keys and said "no thank you" to my whole career because I was so underwater. I learned later that the reason they could not was because they were my restaurant employees, not theirs, therefore it was a breech of our Operator Agreement for them to pay the employees.

However, Woodland Hills had been my dream, and I had learned over the years that sometimes, you have to give a dream a little effort before it comes true. It's not like I had become accustomed to great stuff just falling into my lap. I had learned a lot from my years of struggle—from finding Jesus in high school to putting myself through Oral Roberts University, and from striving to become a successful Chick-fil-A Operator to taking the Eastland and Promenade businesses to new record-setting heights for those restaurants. One foot in front of the other, one day at a time, do your best and let God do the rest. It had worked for me so far…

And it worked again. Once again, I was able to turn things around, to make the most out of the opportunity a high-volume restaurant presented, and eventually to hire better managers…and take better care of them. It was kind of like a snowball… once Woodland Hills got rolling again, it just kept growing.

My family kept growing too, with the addition of Chase in 2000 (this made three if you're counting), and Noell was pregnant again. This could only mean one thing…

It was time for my next challenge.

And I already knew what it would be.

If you were hungry for Chick-fil-A and you lived within an hour and a half radius of Tulsa, there was only one way to satisfy your craving. You had to go to the mall. At that stage, there were no street-located Chick-fil-A restaurants anywhere near the Tulsa area.

My customers had noticed this. They wanted the option of going through a drive-through on their way home from work, or stopping by for a quick bite in the middle of the day, without having to deal with the mall. But Chick-fil-A didn't offer it. Which meant that people were taking their business somewhere else…even when they would rather be eating Chick-fil-A (and who wouldn't?).

To me, this looked like a major opportunity. Tulsa needed a street-located Chick-fil-A restaurant.

I took the idea to the corporate office, but they weren't quite as excited as I was.

Luckily, my odyssey from nowhere kid to successful businessman had taught me another important lesson—no doesn't always mean no.

At least not in business.

So, I set out, as I had so many times, to change the minds of the folks at the home office. I came up with what I thought was a genius plan. I'd get my customers—who I already knew would be very excited about a free-standing Chick-fil-A restaurant- to do my work for me. Whenever someone asked me if there was a free-standing Chick-fil-A restaurant in town, or, more typically, why there *wasn't* a free-standing Chick-fil-A restaurant in town, I handed them a business card for the corporate office and told them to call the company and ask them.

I am assuming some of those customers did call the corporate office. I have no way of knowing for sure, but at one point, I did have someone from the home office ask me to stop.

Apparently, people in Tulsa *were* interested in having a free-standing Chick-fil-A restaurant.

Satisfied that I had made my point, I told the gentleman that I would stop giving the home office card to every Tom, Dick and Harriet who asked about a free-standing Chick-fil-A in Tulsa, *if* they would at least come out, and take a look at the area.

I don't really know if what I did or said made any difference at all, but it did make me feel like I was at least doing something—and I maintain that doing *something* is almost always better than doing nothing. In my mind, it was time for Tulsa to get its first free-standing Chick-fil-A restaurant. And I knew the perfect person to run it…me.

Chick-fil-A, Inc. did send a representative to Tulsa, and ultimately, they did decide to build a free-standing restaurant there. While I was among the "pool" of interested candidates for this new restaurant, there was just one drawback. Only a small number of Chick-fil-A Operators have two or more restaurant businesses because the Chick-fil-A franchise model really revolves around their franchised operators being hands-on, making sure the food and the service is top-notch and being the foundation of the brand.

For me, this meant I would have to give up the Woodland Hills Mall store.

The store was doing amazing business, which was a hard thing to walk away from. But there was more to it than that. The Woodland Hills Mall store really was *my* store — it was the place where I first worked for Chick-fil-A back when I was still in college, it was the store I initially wanted, and it got me into Chick-fil-A as a Business Intern. It was the store I had really turned around and turned into my biggest success so far. How could I give it up — even in pursuit of a bigger dream?

I decided that maybe, given my record of success so far, I wouldn't have to give it up. I set up a dinner with a Chick-fil-A, Inc. vice president, with Noell on hand to back me up and remind him of the leader I was, to talk about the possibility of my joining the elite rank of multi-location Operators. When the vice president explained why they don't recommend running two stores, Noell leapt to my defense, reminding him of my past successes and of how, no matter what the odds, I always managed to increase sales and make a name for myself.

I don't make a practice of letting my wife fight my battles, but as every husband knows deep down inside, it's kind of cool to have your wife stick up for you and show the world how proud she is of you!

Still, after speaking to the vice president for a while, I actually became concerned myself. My stated mission at the time was to "develop leaders in business, life, and Christ!" I had never run a free-standing restaurant — so would I really be able to handle the job if I had two stores?

We prayed about it, and felt God leading me to let Woodland Hills go.

Why? Well, I spent a lot of time thinking about it, praying about it and asking God what to do. Ultimately, He showed me which path to take. All I had to do was listen and follow His lead. And I did.

It was the best decision I ever made. Getting Tulsa's first Chick-fil-A free-standing restaurant up and running was more than a major opportunity, it was a major undertaking. I would be marketing to an entirely different set of consumers and dealing with a whole different set of challenges. If this new opportunity was going to fly, it needed my undivided attention. It deserved all the love and attention I could give it. Of course, in Greeno fashion, Noell had baby #4, Cameron, July 31st, two months before the grand opening of our free-standing restaurant.

With this new free-standing store now my sole responsibility (at least professionally!), I decided it was time for some major marketing stunts to put this quick-service newcomer on the map. Since we were located in Tulsa, Oklahoma — smack dab in the middle of cow country — I could think of no better occasion than the chain's Cow Appreciation Day. Which was, to the rest of the world, simply known as a Friday in July.

If you've ever seen any Chick-fil-A advertising, you know the menu may be all about the chicken, but when it comes to marketing, cows are king. In fact, much of the advertising features cows encouraging folks to "Eat Mor Chikin" (apparently cows are not great spellers).

Cow Appreciation Day is not a national holiday or anything — it's a made-up day created by the brilliant minds at the Chick-fil-A, Inc. marketing department. Basically, the way it works is that anyone who comes in to a Chick-fil-A restaurant dressed like a cow gets a free meal, and anyone partially dressed in cow attire gets a free sandwich — on that day only.

Well, the concept of Cow Appreciation Day caused me to say, "I have an IDEA!" (a phrase that, to this day, still sends a shudder through my marketing crew). I called the corporate office and asked if anyone had ever marketed on Cow Appreciation Day using real cows. Despite their discouragements, I moved forward with the plan anyway.

I built a corral and filled it with hay, and a farmer friend of mine brought six dairy cows to my store. It was a huge hit—pretty soon, hundreds of kids had crowded my parking lot, feeding the cows... and more importantly, eating my chicken!

That is, until Animal Control showed up—along with a news crew.

I felt like I was on an episode of Cops. These two uniformed officers came running up, camera crew right behind them, demanding to see my permit for the cows.

Um...permit? What permit?

One thing I've learned about myself over the years is, I'd rather ask for forgiveness than permission. It's a lot more exciting and a lot more fun! So while Animal Control hitched up my homemade corral, hay and all, and hauled it and my half-dozen cows away, I took advantage of the news crew and gave them an interview—with my son Connor, who happened to be dressed in our cow costume, by my side. When it aired, it was a great piece—it even won some kind of award!

And it wasn't the last time my store would be featured on the evening news.

Since that day, that free-standing restaurant has been Ground Zero for wacky, food-related events in Tulsa, from Guinness World Records to parking lot celebrations to all-night parties. Back at the home office, people may roll their eyes whenever I call, wondering what crazy stunt I'm planning to pull off this time—but they also know it works. It keeps Chick-fil-A in people's minds...as well as their stomachs! And it makes the emotional connections that are so important to turning customers into lifelong fans.

The result? Well, when I was given sales projections from the corporate office on what they hoped for, we were able to hit the third-year goals by the end of the second year. We easily surpassed all sales expectations.

And my family? Well, that kept growing too. But in 2004, Noell gave birth to who we thought would be our fifth and final child, a little girl we named Savannah. Five kids were what we wanted, what we planned for and what we had. So I had a vasectomy.

But God, apparently, had other plans... and a sense of humor!

The whole idea behind a vasectomy is that it basically eliminates any chance of having kids. The procedure's not a lot of fun and can be scary, but it's definitely worth it.

So imagine how I felt in 2005, when Noell told me she was pregnant again.

How could that possibly have happened?

I went back to the doctor, who told me that there was one way and *only* one way that this could have happened. My beloved wife, my wonderful Noell, was having an affair.

Seriously? *My Noell?*

Clearly, the doctor did not understand how totally irresistible I am to my wife. Or at least, he failed to see what an amazing, honest, trustworthy person she is. But while he may have doubted her, I never did. I went to another doctor for a second opinion, and he discovered the reason for Noell's seemingly Immaculate Conception.

I actually had a third tube that the vasectomy didn't take care of. No wonder I had so many kids—my reproductive system was like a superhighway! And even though I thought I had shut it down, my little baby making dudes still managed to find a way through. Apparently, having six kids was part of God's plan for the Greenos. In fact, a few years before, when she was pregnant with Baby #4, our friend Darci Cahill told Noell that she'd had a vision that we would have six children. Four boys and two girls. Noell said, OK, that's fine, because we plan on adopting. Darci said, no, I feel these are yours.

Luckily, she didn't say seven. I had a *second* vasectomy...and so far, so good.

But God wasn't quite done with me yet—when it comes to my life, the Big Guy definitely seems to have a wicked sense of humor. With Noell pregnant and juggling five kids, I learned that the Operator of the Woodland Hills Mall restaurant was leaving for another store in Texas. I had to apply, just like before, but I was more seasoned, and ready, and they came around.

So, as Noell prepared to give birth to our sixth child, a girl named Sydney, I returned to the Woodland Hills store. I was now the franchised Operator of two Chick-fil-A restaurant businesses, a father of six, and husband to a smokin' hot — and very patient — woman.

I had a pretty great life. And I still do.

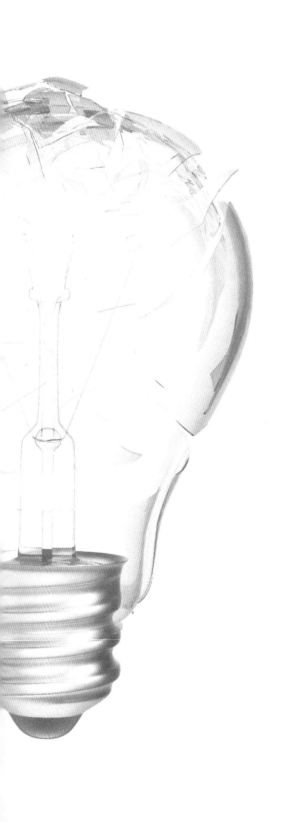

CHAPTER 12
WHAT WILL YOU DO WITH YOUR STORY?

Everyone wants to be a part of something bigger than him or herself.

- Arthur Greeno

I t is amazing to see how everyone really does want to be a part of something bigger.

That's why every event I do, it's not just me doing it. Its lots and lots of others. I like to give the community an opportunity to get involved.

When we made the world's largest lemonade, we had dozens of customers squeezing some of our 11,000+ lemons in order to make it fresh-squeezed resulting in a Guinness world-record and raising $10,000 for the Little Light House, a local school for disabled children.

At Christmas we set up a deal for our customers to purchase Chick-fil-A box meals for the homeless shelter. We in turn would deliver them out to the shelter. It's an easy way for customers to touch people's lives, providing over 4,100 meals last year at the shelters.

When we set the record for the world's largest sweet tea, we put over 3,500 lbs of ice in the huge cup. We had every person at that event help: we made a long line of about 100 people to help us move each 12x12 block of ice, so they could lay claim to helping set a world record.

If you're not sure that everyone wants to be a part of something bigger, here are two stories involving the same person.

Danny Cahill was 450 lbs at his biggest point in life. Then he entered *The Biggest Loser*. Danny, his wife Darci, Noell and I have known each other for a few years, as Noell was in the choir with Danny. Danny told us he was selected to be on *The Biggest Loser*. So we thought it would be cool to get some people rooting for him.It just so happened that we were at the release of the new Star Trek movie (I know, you're surprised I'm a trekkie). It was full theater, over 400+ people. I went down to the front, got everyone's attention, and told them all how Danny got selected for the show, and would be on TV. I gave the audience his cell phone number, so that they could text him some home-town encouragement. He was just finishing packing at home, and his phone went berserk: it started chirping, and vibrating, texts were coming so fast he could not press the buttons to look at the text before the next one beeped. This went on for almost 300 messages within a 10 minute span. They did not know Danny, never even heard of him, but they wanted to be a part of something big. (In addition to the movie theater, we also did an email and mass text to all our friends. In total, his phone went off over 700 times that day.)

This is a quote from one of Danny's articles, talking about how you need someone to help you succeed:

> "… When I landed and showed up at my coming home party, I was greeted by another partner…my wife. I had bought her a bracelet and was going to ask her to renew our vows. She had stood by me through thick and thin and I wanted her to know that she would be standing by me in the end. The help my wife gave me was immense. She did whatever it took to encourage me and help me get the workouts in. She had cleaned out the cabinets and had good food in the kitchen. She did everything she had to do to 'hold me up' just like they did at that seminar. But there was another partner. That partner was Arthur and Noell Greeno.

Like they did in the beginning, they provided help again while I was home. They thought to themselves, "What can we contribute to Danny and Darci that will help make this journey easier and more successful?" The answer was Arthur's ability to lead, organize and administrate. When a task has to be done and most people ask themselves, "Can we really do this?" Arthur would ask himself, "Why couldn't we do this?" He can take large things and make them relatively simple...that is his gift. So when the bills kept coming in and I had quit my job to focus on winning *The Biggest Loser*, the envelopes began coming. Arthur and Noell reached out to their network of friends and asked them to not only contribute, but to reach out to their networks, too. "We have a friend in need," they said, "They need our help! Anything you can give, give!" People were sending him checks of $5, $10, $100, and more! Some that couldn't give simply sent cards of encouragement which were just as important as finances! They knew that people generally want to be a part of something BIG! The people gave anything they could. They gave more than just money. When I needed a gas grill on which to cook my skinless, boneless chicken breast, Arthur and Noell put the word out and found a donor! When I needed a freezer to hold my skinless, boneless chicken breasts, Arthur brought a freezer! When a bill would come in and Darci and I didn't know how we were going to pay it, a phone call would come! "We've got another envelope for you, Danny." It never failed that at the last minute, my needs were met; because I had help.

To this day I have a stack of cards that came with the support from Arthur and Noell's friends while we were struggling to finish the race of *The Biggest Loser*. I often read them. They provide a reminder that no one person can "go it alone" without a team of support. I will never forget the help that Darci, Arthur and Noell and their network of supporters, Liz, and numerous others provided me! They can all share in my *Biggest Loser* story; after all, when I stood on that scale on December 8th, 2009, I stood with every person that helped, prayed, and encouraged me. It wasn't just Danny Cahill on that scale but it was a group of "partners" that were about to be crowned The Biggest Loser ever...and I will ever be indebted to them all.

There is a scripture in the Bible that speaks of this. It is Ecclesiastes 4:9-10 which says, "Two are better than one, because they have a good return for their labor: If either of them falls down, one can help the other up. But pity anyone who falls and has no one to help them up." This speaks to me so well. We all need *partners* in life. We all need *help* in situations we are in. And I can honestly say that without people like Darci, Arthur and Liz, my path on *The Biggest Loser* would have been a much harder path to follow; and it may have lead to second place instead of being The Biggest Loser ever on that show! I thank God for my partners every day. And I am always looking for more partners as well as more people who need a partner! I ask you one question: *Who's helping you?*"[1]

I was able to connect Danny to others, giving them an opportunity to bless the Cahill family, in turn blessing the givers, and the receivers. In the end, he has been able to influence millions of people. Danny lost 239lbs to win that year's *The Biggest Loser*, and to date, he is The Biggest Loser ever.

At my restaurants, after someone has worked for two weeks, I show them a Chick-fil-A video. It's called Every Person Has a Story. It has no talking, and pans around a Chick-fil-A restaurant slowly. As it comes across guests or workers, it has subtitles. One guest comes up to the register and the words say "fired from his job, worried about how to provide for his family." Then it

---

slowly moves to another man: "after fighting cancer, he is recently diagnosed cancer-free." Then to a little girl with an icecream cone: "mom died during childbirth, dad blames her." Then to a college-aged cashier: "worked through high school, now accepted to the college of her dreams."

What I ask is, "If every person has a story, what part do you have in their story?"

As hard as my story was, there were many who had a great part in making me what I am today. If others were to tell their story, and you were in it, what would it look like?

What does your story say?

No matter where you are in life, beginning or end, you are the one who gets to choose what doors you walk through, how hard you try, and who you influence. It's never too early, or too late to start. If they can do it, why can't you?

Tiger Woods was three years old when he shot 48 for 9 holes in golf.

Mozart was 8 when he wrote his first symphony.

Michael Jackson was 9 when he released his first album.

Fu Mingxia is a diver and was an Olympic gold medalist at 13 years old.

Ralph Waldo Emerson was 14 when he enrolled at Harvard.

Paul McCartney was 15 when John Lennon invited him to join his band.

Bill Gates was 19 when he co-founded Microsoft.

Plato was 20 when he became a student of Socrates.

S. Truett Cathy was 25 when he and his brother Ben first started the Dwarf House later to become Chick-fil-A.

Joe Dimaggio was 26 when he hit safely in 56 consecutive games.

William Shakespeare was 31 when he wrote *Romeo and Juliet*.

Bill Gates was 31 when he became a billionaire.

Thomas Jefferson was 33 when he wrote the *Declaration of Independence.*

Arthur Greeno was 39 when he achieved his first world record.

Danny Cahill was 40 when he decided to go from 430 lbs to 191 lbs to be The Biggest Loser ever on NBC's *The Biggest Loser.*

Jack Nicklaus was 46 when he shot 65 in the final round, and 30 on the back nine, to win the masters.

Henry Ford was 50 when he started his first assembly line.

Ray Kroc was a 52-year-old milkshake machine salesmen when he bought out Mac and Dick McDonald and officially started McDonald's.

Walt Disney was 55 when he opened Magic Kingdom.

Dom Perignon was 60 when he first produced champagne.

Oscar Hammerstein II was 64 when he wrote the lyrics for *The Sound of Music.*

Winston Churchhill was 65 when he became Britain's prime minister

Michelangelo was 72 when he designed the dome of St. Peter's Basilica in Rome.

John Glenn was 77 years old on his last mission to outer space.

Frank Lloyd Wright was 91 when he completed his work on the Guggenheim Museum.

George Moyse took his first skydive at the age of 97.

Dimitrion Yourdanidis was 98 years old when he ran a marathon in 7 hours and 39 minutes in Athens, Greece.

Ichijirou Araya was 100 when he climbed Mount Fuji.

ACKNOWLEDGEMENTS

Throughout my life so many people have influenced me, and they don't even know it. They were a big part of my story.

My Savior Jesus Christ, who saw me for who I was, and still died for me, knowing who I will eventually be.

Stan Lee—Author of *Spiderman*, *X-men*, and *Iron Man*—when my life was hard and I was battling at a young age, most of the time we had no T.V. so I was emersed in comic books. I would see how sometimes normal people could do super things. However, they still had to do what is right to defeat those who could not.

Youth pastors—when I was in my early teens they showed me God's love and acceptance, helping me learn about the Christian walk.

Walt Disney—in college, I learned to use my creativity, and if you have ever been to a Disney park, it's amazing to see how they use creativity.

S. Truett Cathy—his was the success story of a businessman I wanted to be. A great Christian who is smart in business, he gives back to others and helps them reach their dreams.

Others included the groundskeeper for the waterfall, Bob and Carol Cleaver.

Darrell Cleaver, Mark Collier, and Mike Tedford—you guys rock!!

People who I rode with to church when I had no ride, maintenance workers who influenced me at Silver Birch Ranch, Jack and Lynda Connor... The list goes on and on.

My wife Noell, my best friend, you inspire me daily to be a better man. You are the reason I told my story, since for most my life I thought my past was "my crap, and no one wanted to hear it!" I will love no one else like you, you are my lobster.

Connor, Casey, Chase, Cameron, Savannah, and Syd — the reason I wrote this was two-fold. One, I did not want to repeat it 6 times. The other reason is, I want you to achieve more than I do, and know that nothing will hold you back. I love you all.

Thank you to all of my friends for pushing me to get this done — Danny Cahill, Netboy Veit, Rob Clyatt.

Thanks to my team, that runs our restaurants so well, I can take time to do crazy marketing and write a book. Lorine and Robert Martinez, John Stewart, Cathy Mcnew, She-Ra Ford, Christine Rand, Chris Mickle, Jenn Gristani, and all my team.

Thank you to my family, Dad, Mom, Lorine, and Kathleen, for making every day an adventure!

Basically, if they did not pour into my life, then I would not have been able to share my successes with you. So, whose life will you pour into? You could be that little push they need to get them to greatness, and they could be the catalyst you need to take your life to new heights. Never underestimate what your impact on others could be.

Arthur Greeno speaks to thousands of people a year on these topics:

♦ The heart of Customer Service — How does his team care for customers on a personal level.

♦ Extreme Marketing — Multiple Guinness world record holder, listed in the *Ripley's Believe It or Not* books. He has been written up in the *New York Times*, as well as countless local papers, newscasts, and other local media. He has helped raise tens of thousands of dollars for organizations like The Little Light House, and every year feeds thousands of people who are in need.

♦ Dysfunctional Inspiration — His story of overcoming incredible odds to find his backroads journey to success.

Arthur also volunteers his time for the organization The Journey Training, that helps people reach their greatness. www.thejourneytraining.com

For more information:
Contact him at www.arthurgreeno.com